Florida A&M University, Tallahassee
Florida Atlantic University, Boca Raton
Florida Gulf Coast University, Ft. Myers
Florida International University, Miami
Florida State University, Tallahassee
University of Central Florida, Orlando
University of Florida, Gainesville
University of North Florida, Jacksonville
University of South Florida, Tampa
University of West Florida, Pensacola

Larry Roberts

Florida's

University Press of Florida

Gainesville » Tallahassee » Tampa » Boca Raton

Pensacola » Orlando » Miami » Jacksonville » Ft. Myers

Golden Age of Souvenirs

1890–1930

06 05 04 03 02 01 6 5 4 3 2 1

Library of Congress Cataloging-in-Publication Data
Roberts, Larry, 1946-
Florida's golden age of souvenirs, 1890-1930 / Larry Roberts.
p. cm.
Includes bibliographical references and index.
ISBN 0-8130-2424-2 (alk. paper)
1. Florida—Collectibles. 2. Souvenirs (Keepsakes)—Collectors and
collecting—Florida. I. Title.
NK5045 .R63 2001
975.9'0075—DC21 2001027595

The University Press of Florida is the scholarly publishing agency for the
State University System of Florida, comprising Florida A&M University,
Florida Atlantic University, Florida Gulf Coast University, Florida Interna-
tional University, Florida State University, University of Central Florida,
University of Florida, University of North Florida, University of South
Florida, and University of West Florida.

University Press of Florida
15 Northwest 15th Street
Gainesville, FL 32611–2079
http://www.upf.com

Contents

Acknowledgments

First, I'd like to thank my parents, Courtnay and Margaret Roberts, for igniting my interest in history and for then supporting and encouraging me from my first fossil shark's tooth to my last alligator cane. A special thanks to my dear wife, Jeannie, for managing our business so I could pursue my research and ultimately write this book, and for the many hours she spent translating and transcribing my handwritten text to type. A note of gratitude to my son, Josh, for his good humor and unselfish support.

Beyond the family to the family of friends, a heartfelt thanks to the following people: Alice Hinson for her keen eye in editing my book and her kind words of encouragement, Stan Blomeley for the many hours spent photographing my collection, the staff of the Matheson Historical Center for help and access to their fine collection of Florida books, to research librarians Glenn Emory and Lewis Zeleaka at the Jacksonville Public Library's Florida collection for their help and acute knowledge of available resources. Thanks also to the staff at P. K. Yonge Library at the University of Florida, the Museum of Florida History, and the St. Augustine Historical Society. I wish to thank Steve Werts for his help in directing me to the University Press of Florida and express my gratitude to the gracious and competent staff who helped my book to fruition. An extended thanks to other libraries, historical societies, and institutions that helped me along the way.

Finally I'd like to recognize my fellow collectors for their encouragement and shared research, in particular, Tom Staley, Bob Carr, Dr. Fred Frankel, Dan McKenna, Jerry and Beth Bowan, Ken Breslauer, Ty and Jean Tyson, Mike Turberville, and Doug Hendriksen.

Abbreviations

The following abbreviations appear in the captions of the figures and plates.
All group shots are described left to right or top to bottom.

b	bottom
b.	back
c	center
ca.	circa
cat.	catalogue
cvd.	carved
d.	diameter
emb.	embossed
enm.	enameled
f	front
G&C	Greenleaf & Crosby
h.	height
han.	handle
l	left
mkd.	marked
r	right
S & P	salt & pepper
t	top
WWI	World War I

Introduction

Being a native Floridian, I have always been fascinated by alligators. When I first started collecting Florida souvenirs about twenty years ago, I was primarily looking for carved alligator canes. Their folksy charm and fanciful representations appealed to my naturalist bent. As I developed the collection, I began noticing carved alligator pipes, then carved alligator inkwells. I soon realized that there was an amazing selection of gator-related souvenirs and began expanding my collection. As the menagerie grew, I became infatuated with Florida souvenirs as a whole. A few years ago it occurred to me that others might like to visit my collection through pictures and perhaps find out something new along the way.

Most of what I write about here falls into what I call the "Golden Age of Souvenirs," which lasted from about 1890 to about 1930. This forty-year period saw a rising national passion for souvenirs that directly coincided with Florida's popularity as a booming tourist destination. Millions of souvenirs were sold throughout the state, leaving the industrious collector an incredible legacy of fun and discovery.

Florida's two biggest businesses have always been tourism and agriculture. Because industry has played only a small part in the state's past, Florida souvenirs are among the few remaining objects that can be found in great enough numbers to make collecting worthwhile. They also give us a tangible link to history, for instance, pictorial souvenirs like scenic china join us visually to Florida's past.

Florida's Golden Age of Souvenirs provides a cumulative look at Florida memorabilia. It not only covers well-documented mementos like scenic china and souvenir spoons, but it also looks at lesser-known items like orangewood carvings and shieldware figurines. A few chapters stray outside the Golden Age time frame, in order to follow the complete evolution of certain local souvenirs. Postcards and paper ephemera will only be covered in conjunction with other souvenirs. I have avoided the area of paper souvenirs, because this aspect of Floridiana deserves a book of its own.

Florida's long relationship with the tourist-souvenir trade has given us a wonderful variety of keepsakes. They tell the story of our state's heritage and bridge the past to the present in fascinating ways that nothing else can. This book offers the casual browser along with the budding collector an informal yet enlightening introduction to the diverse and rewarding hobby of collecting old Florida souvenirs.

A Historical Sketch
of Florida Tourism

Since tourism was the industry that would ultimately create Florida's souvenir trade, a brief historical sketch of tourism's developmental years, roughly 1830–1930, should be useful.

Originally, there were three groups that formed the greater body of tourists. The first to arrive were invalids. Leisure tourists and sportsmen would follow, but it would not be until after the Civil War, that is, from about 1866 on, that they would have their biggest impact.

Before becoming a U.S. territory in 1821, Florida had seen little development. It was hardly more than a military backwater under Spanish rule for nearly four hundred years. Although the British would own Florida from 1763 to 1783, the land would ultimately return to Spain and to the status quo. There were only two towns of consequence, St. Augustine and Pensacola, both decaying bastions of Spain's fading colonial empire. When Florida joined the union in 1821, the United States acquired eight hundred miles of panhandle and peninsula from the boundary of Florida and Alabama to Key West. For the most part, it was unexplored and unexploited, a lost and lawless land.

By the 1830s steamboats became the primary mode of transportation along Florida's coasts and rivers. Government snag boats began clearing obstacles from the prominent waterways and would soon open the territory's remote

Figure 2.1 Trade card illustrating Florida's natural and historical attractions, ca. 1880–1890.

interior. As a result, the St. Johns River would become the major artery to Florida's heartland.

Because of the Second Seminole war, 1835–1842, all of northeast Florida would remain a remote and unhealthy destination for travelers, with two exceptions, St. Augustine and Jacksonville, both well protected by American militia. It would be St. Augustine's Old World charm that would entice Florida's first tourists. By the 1830s this quaint Spanish settlement, defined by its Moorish architecture, old forts, and secure environs, would become Florida's primary destination for weary New England visitors. The fresh air and winter warmth of this insular community soon began attracting a seasonal influx of invalids. The locals called them "strangers."

In 1834, St. Augustine would have six boarding houses to accommodate its visitors. In contrast, Jacksonville offered limited accommodations, completing its first hotel a decade later. However, its prime location near the mouth of Florida's longest navigable river, the St. Johns, would soon establish Jacksonville as Florida's gateway city.

By 1845, the Savannah Line ran regular trips by steamship from Savannah to Jacksonville. Invalids continued their winter pilgrimage to St. Augustine, as Jacksonville developed its own accommodations. By 1851 Jacksonville boasted three new hotels, attracting leisure tourists as well as the standard health-seekers. Trips down the picturesque St. Johns became the major attraction, as comfortable river steamers gave tourists a firsthand look at Florida's terra incognita.

Yet, just as the promising tourist trade was getting underway, disaster struck. The Civil War, from 1861 to 1865, would return Florida to its old military status, and the tourist trade would collapse as ocean and river steamers were impressed into military service.

Union naval superiority guaranteed a swift occupation of Florida's coastal towns, including St. Augustine, but Jacksonville took the brunt of the war, suffering extensive loss to fire and other damage from regular military conflicts and bombardment, while the Confederacy maintained control of the interior.

But compared with the rest of the embattled South, Florida would emerge relatively unscathed. The land supported little industry other than farming, and the Union chose to concentrate its military power north of the state.

After the war, it was not long before tourists resumed their annual winter treks south, and by the 1870s, existing hotels in Jacksonville and St. Augustine were hard pressed to provide rooms for them all.

New England newspapers and magazines like *Harper's* and *Leslie's* featured articles extolling Florida's appeal as a sunny, exotic, and healthful destination.

Figure 2.2 Photo postcard of tourists enjoying the company of a stuffed gator, ca. 1900–1910. Alligators were popular props in photo studios and often appear in whimsical poses along with a note like "Having a great time in sunny Florida."

Lyrical commentary and crisp engravings illustrated a tropical paradise with thick jungles, lush orange groves, and curious wildlife, beckoning those with independent spirits along with those with depleted constitutions. Florida's prominence at select expositions in the 1890s kept it in the forefront of the potential tourist's mind.

Tour guidebooks were written covering all aspects of an exciting Florida visit, and columnists sent home details of their adventures. The 1890s marked the beginning of the postcard-collecting craze that grew unabated throughout the Golden Age. Satisfied tourists mailed millions of picture postcards from Florida, each with an enticing view and a happy note extolling the virtues of the land of sunshine. Postcards provided free advertisement and plenty of it. By the 1890s Florida had become the leading tourist destination of the United States.

By now, the industrial revolution had changed the face of the Northeast. Coal-burning, steam powered factories left a gray shroud of pollution over congested cities and mill towns.

With the machine age came a prosperous upper class and a fast-developing middle class in the Northeast, all choking on their own industrial spew. A combination of combustive pollution and long, cold winters could result in a congestive disorder known then as consumption and later as tuberculosis. For their consumptive patients' relief, doctors heartily recommended a winter's stay in Florida's warm, curative clime.

Another disorder associated with the machine-driven economy and recommending Florida's tropical tonic was known as broken health or "brain-fag" (brain fatigue). This condition was caused by long hours at work, the schedule pressures of production, and the hectic pace of crowded city life. The Florida remedy promised a sure cure for those ills, no matter how desperate the suf-

Figure 2.3 Jacksonville trade card showing two of the city's largest hotels and Bay Street, ca. 1880–1890.

Florida's Golden Age of Souvenirs

Figure 2.4 Clyde's Steamship Lines brochure, ca. 1880–1890.

ferer. By the 1870s Florida began seeing a greater influx of leisure tourists who had heard the sultry call of the sunny South. Soon they would dominate the tourist industry.

As the machine age moved south, railroads greatly improved and would soon compete with steamboats for the tourist trade. The Atlantic Coast Line Railway had a direct route from Philadelphia to Jacksonville by 1869. First-class ocean steamers left New York, Philadelphia, and Baltimore on regular weekly runs to Savannah with connections by rail and other steamer lines to Jacksonville.

The "Gateway City" had become Florida's leading point of destination for all major steamships and railroad lines. From 1869 to 1879 nine major hotels would be built to accommodate the growing inflow of the nouveau riche. In season, Jacksonville's population would increase fourfold, and the city was soon called the "Winter City in Summerland." From the 1870s until the mid-1880s, Jacksonville would witness an explosion in tourism, not only from the United States but from abroad as well. Henry Lee in his 1886 *Tourist Guide of Florida* noted, "Tourists from every section of the globe are to be met with here among them leading statesmen and representatives of eminence, wealth and fashion . . . together with many of the nobility of Europe."

River steamers provided the greatest diversion, many running the 206-mile circuit south from Jacksonville to Sanford, where Euro-American civilization stopped. Various lines provided daily sightseeing and hunting excursions along the course of the St. Johns, where exotic birds and alligators shared the shoreline. The steamers also visited smaller resorts and health spas, like Magnolia, Green Cove Springs, and Enterprise, where passengers could find refreshment and relaxation. Regular stops were made at the small town of Tocoi; there tourists wishing to see St. Augustine boarded a crude mule-drawn trolley for the jarring fifteen-mile trip. Whether the journey took four or five hours, it was reported, depended on the age and attitude of the mule.

Another popular stop was Palatka, where passengers would connect with the Hart Lines' smaller steamers for the popular Ocklawaha and Silver Springs tours and riverboat hunting trips. From there, Sanford, on Lake Monroe, was the final destination before the larger steamers returned to Jacksonville.

Figure 2.5 Business card from the Clarendon, Green Cove Springs, ca. 1880–1890.

Florida's Golden Age of Souvenirs

Figure 2.6 Postcard of the Magnolia Hotel two miles above Green Cove Springs, ca. 1900–1910, built in 1851, one of the earliest on the St. Johns River.

Figure 2.7 Tocoi railroad depot, ca. 1870–1880.

PALATKA, FLORIDA.

SEASON

1890.

H. L.

HART'S

DAILY

LINE.

OCKLAWAHA RIVER STEAMERS.

STEAMER OKEEHUMKEE   STEAMER OSCEOLA,
      CAPT. A. N. EDWARDS.   CAPT. H. A. GRAY.

STEAMER ASTATULA,   STEAMER MARION,
      CAPT. D. A. DUNHAM.   CAPT. W. H. HARRISON.

For Schedule see all Ticket Agents.   H. L. HART, Gen'l Manager.

Figure 2.8 Ocklawaha River Steamer promotional card, 1890.

Around the 1890s shooting from the decks of steamboats was discouraged by the captains, as wildlife along the St. Johns and Ocklawaha Rivers was fast disappearing. Nevertheless, the remote headwaters and lakes of the St. Johns just south of Sanford provided the sportsman with incredible hunting opportunities. Here, alligators covered the riverbanks and clouds of ducks and geese blackened the sky. Hunting trips could be arranged in Sanford, where guides and their smaller, more adaptable steamboats could be hired.

By the mid 1880s, tourism on Florida's east coast would undergo a dramatic change. In 1884, Henry Flagler, one of the founders of Standard Oil, visited St. Augustine and was charmed by its Old World atmosphere, but he found the accommodations less to his taste. Accustomed to New England's grand hotels, Flagler viewed St. Augustine's rooms as small and primitive in comparison. A man with visionary business insight and immense wealth, he saw the potential of building elegant hotels for an exceedingly wealthy northern clientele. He also realized the importance of quick and reliable transportation to these hotels, and he began purchasing local railroads to ensure direct and dependable rail service. Nearing retirement at fifty-three, he turned his energies and resources toward his ambitious revitalization of St. Augustine and the regional railroads.

In 1885, Flagler began building the Ponce de Leon Hotel, and by 1888 he had witnessed its remarkably successful grand opening. The elegant Moorish architecture, exquisite furnishings, and superb cuisine would set the standards for future Flagler hotels. In 1889, Flagler had completed the Alcazar adjacent to the Ponce de Leon, and in the same year, he purchased the Cordova. With his work in St. Augustine complete, he would focus on his march south along

Florida's Golden Age of Souvenirs

the desolate eastern seaboard. As his rails moved down the coast on his newly formed Florida East Coast Railroad, so did his grand hotels.

In 1890, Flagler would open the recently acquired and remodeled Ormond Hotel, near Daytona, whose population at the time was a scant three hundred people. In 1894, Palm Beach would welcome the Royal Poinciana Hotel, followed by the Palm Beach Inn, later called the Breakers. Flager's railroad arrived in Miami in 1896, and the Royal Palm Hotel was under construction that same year. Miami's population at the time was a little more than 1,500. Yet Flagler was already planning his greatest venture—to span the open sea to his final destination, Key West. The completion of Flagler's railway from Miami to Key West in 1912 represented one of the greatest engineering feats of the time. The entire eastern seaboard of Florida from Jacksonville to Key West and Cuba became the winter playground for presidents, European royalty, and affluent Americans.

Flagler's luxurious hotels offered the best in American accommodations, places where patrons could mix with the elite and flaunt their newfound wealth. Florida had become the American Riviera and an international playground. Meanwhile, Henry Plant, another Florida entrepreneur, was actively establishing his own rail line, modestly called the Plant System. Pushing south through the central part of the state and along the Gulf Coast, Plant's railroad would soon dominate existing rail companies. Through buyouts and business maneuvers for which he would become notorious, he would extend his railroad

Figure 2.9 St. Augustine's Cordova Hotel advertising booklet, ca. 1880–1890.

from Jacksonville to Sanford and Tampa by 1892. The Plant System also included steamship lines that served Tampa, Florida's west coast, and Cuba.

In 1891, Plant completed the exotic Tampa Bay Hotel, with its distinctive Moorish minarets. This uniquely elegant structure with an equally opulent interior assured Tampa its position as the predominant destination on the Gulf Coast. In 1897, Plant would open the Belleview Biltmore Hotel in Belleair, just south of Clearwater, to rave reviews and resounding success. By the time of Plant's death in 1899, he would own eight hotels in central Florida and on Florida's west coast. The development of hotels and other accommodations along the Gulf Coast focused on attracting wealthy Midwestern industrialists and financiers, who chose this region as their preferred playground.

As the railroads continued moving south, tourists found the hitherto inaccessible interior and sparsely settled coasts were opening to reveal Florida's sunlit secrets. Soon, small towns began to appear along the many rail lines, accompanied by new hotels, resorts, and health spas.

In 1845, Florida had one operating railroad that ran 21 miles from Tallahassee to St. Mark's. By 1870, 537 miles of railroad existed, and by 1905, 3,500 miles, quite an impressive development. Florida's continued transportation growth would ensure an ever increasing flood of tourists until the United States entered World War I in 1916. With the country at war, there was little time for Florida vacations. Nevertheless, Florida would become a refuge for wealthy Europeans temporarily escaping from the ravages of war.

By the end of hostilities, Florida would see a new wave of rich industrialists who prospered as a result of the war. The stage was set for the Roaring Twenties and another tourist boom, this time centering in Miami.

The advent of mass-produced automobiles in 1914 gave Americans a new and cheaper form of transportation, and thousands made their way to Florida after the war. Florida's accessibility to the country's largest population centers—the East and Midwest—along with a new American prosperity found the state overrun not only with tourists, but with land speculators as well. Most headed for Miami. America's last great land rush was on. From 1920 to 1925, Miami's population more than doubled, from 29,571 to 69,754. The state's population grew by 30 percent, and Miami Beach, which had been a deserted barrier island until 1915, would see fifty-four new hotels by 1925.

Many fortunes were made, but the boom mentality and the speculative euphoria had forced Florida land to artificially high prices that would implode by 1926. The financial disaster ominously foreshadowed the arrival of the Great Depression and a dramatic decline in Florida tourism.

As Florida staggered under the weight of financial collapse, nature would deliver the final blow, literally. Two devastating hurricanes would hit Florida, one in 1926, destroying 2,000 homes in Miami and 1,500 in Ft. Lauderdale, and another in 1928, killing two thousand people on Lake Okeechobee.

By 1929, all of America was feeling the full effect of the Great Depression. Thousands of banks failed, stocks lost most of their value, and unemployment was over 50 percent. The financial shock waves were felt worldwide. The Depression lasted ten years, until World War II revived American industry and ultimately Florida tourism.

The hundred-year evolution of tourism, 1830–1930, thus saw Florida change from a distant wilderness territory to a bustling tourist Eden. Defined by its unspoiled beauty and tropical warmth, Florida would be pulled into the developing world by a growing tourist trade based on accommodating cold Yankees in search of winter warmth.

The Atlantic and Gulf Coasts would simultaneously see radical changes, as railroads and the development they spawned changed the face of Florida. Many new buildings would embrace the Mediterranean style, inspired by Florida's Spanish heritage and reinvented by Flagler and Plant architects. The east and west coasts would draw tourists from two distinct geographic locations. Florida's east coast drew its tourists from the Eastern Seaboard, while travelers from the Midwest chose the Gulf Coast. Florida's rapid development paralleled the evolving tourist trade and set the groundwork for an industry that today is the heartbeat of Florida's economy.

Florida Souvenirs

Florida is often associated with the whimsical souvenirs that covered the shelves of tourist stands in the 1950s and 1960s.

With World War II over, a new peace and prosperity would find millions of happy visitors pouring into Florida looking for fun, sun, and souvenirs. Cheap, mass-produced mementos featuring flamingos, alligators, and palm trees soon found their way into thousands of American homes. Plastic, plaster, and ceramics reigned, as cheap keepsakes became tokens of working-class vacations.

Because of their relatively new postwar origins, and Florida's successful revival as a tourist state, many baby boomers would see cheap souvenirs as a Florida trademark. Today, they have gained renewed popularity as high kitsch in the pop market for counterculture collectibles. Unfortunately, the familiarity of these later twentieth-century Florida souvenirs has tended to overshadow earlier examples. These differ from the often preconceived ideas of Florida memorabilia and may reflect a part of Florida unfamiliar to most people.

To keep things in perspective and to better understand the origin of Florida souvenirs, we need to start at the beginning, around 1830. About this time, as St. Augustine welcomed Florida's first trickle of winter guests, mostly invalids from the Northeast, it is safe to speculate that enterprising locals would recognize a captive market for their crafts and natural curiosities. Apart from such assumptions, there is little to indicate exactly when the souvenir trade began in St. Augustine.

The typical three-month visit to "America's Oldest Town" provided little entertainment, other than an introductory trip to the beach and breakfast-to-lunch jaunts around town. As tourists became familiar with their surroundings, they undoubtedly visited the local souvenir stands, buying seashells, exotic bird feathers, alligator teeth, and other bio-curios. With Darwinian doctrine fashionably infusing Victorian intellect, natural science had become a popular hobby among Florida visitors.

One could assume that tourists with dawning scientific curiosities would enjoy whiling away the hours by seeking items of intrigue for their developing specimen collections. What better place than the untouched Florida wilderness, with its amazing variety of unique animal and plant life? If natural science failed to interest the tourists, they could purchase locally produced bonnets, hats, and fans that were woven with palmetto fronds and traditionally made by locals of Minorcan descent. Later, these artisans would make baskets, trays, and small utilitarian containers, as demand inspired variety. Dewhurst noted in 1881, "The many girls and young ladies dressed with neatness and task, and many earn the means to support themselves by braiding palmetto for hats and baskets, making feather flowers, shell and fishscale ornaments, and bouquets of native grasses." Braided palmetto souvenirs continued to be popular well into the twentieth century.

Figure 3.1 Palmetto hat factory postcard, ca. 1900–1910.

ISAIAH GREEGOR,
MANUFACTURER AND DEALER IN
FLORIDA JEWELRY, CURIOSITIES, GRASSES,
AND
RARE SHELLS
Orders by Mail Promptly Attended to.
89 DUVAL STREET,
JACKSONVILLE, FLORIDA.
P. O. BOX 717.
(OVER)

Figure 3.2 Business card of Isaiah Greegor, in business in Jacksonville, 1883–1884.

By the mid 1840s, Jacksonville and other small towns along the St. Johns River had begun developing facilities to accommodate a rapidly growing tourist trade that would prove a boon to Florida's budding economy. Natural curiosities maintained their popularity until well after the Civil War. Jacksonville's continued growth following Reconstruction and its favorable location on the St. Johns River led to its ultimate domination of the postwar tourist industry and souvenir trade.

In 1876, the popular lyricist Sidney Lanier visited Jacksonville while compiling information for a tourist guidebook. He describes Jacksonville's bustling Bay Street, where "visitors are trooping everywhere . . . to the fruit stores, to the palmetto braiders, to the curiosity shops. . . . The visitor strolling down this street soon discovers that not an inconsiderable item in the commerce of Jacksonville is the trade in 'Florida curiosities,' to which he will find several establishments devoted. These curiosities are sea-beans, alligator's teeth, plumes of herons and curlew's feathers, crane's wings, angel fish, mangrove and orange[wood] walking canes, coral branches, coquina figurines, and many others." He also notes, "The alligator teeth are made into whistles, watch charms, and the like." Local taxidermists added to the spectacle with salesroom menageries of stuffed alligators, animals, and birds. Bay Street became so well known for its specialty shops that it was commonly called "Curio Row."

Though Jacksonville claimed much of the curio trade, St. Augustine could not be dismissed. A Florida visit was incomplete without embracing the charms of "America's Oldest City," with its numerous arcades and souvenir shops along King and St. George Streets. One tourist noted in 1880, "Even the Indians detained at Fort Marion . . . employed their time making bows and arrows and polishing seabeans . . . which they sold to visitors at the fort." An 1885

"Tourist Edition" supplement from a local periodical, *The Naturalist in Florida*, offers a defining look at keepsakes sold in St. Augustine at the time. An advertisement for the "Fort Marion Store" listed a variety of curiosities including jewelry made from alligator teeth, sea beans, shells, and fish scales. Other novelties such as large "liver beans" with engraved Florida scenes, canes, orangewood paper cutters, stuffed alligators, and alligator purses were featured as well. Natural curios also included "shells from the Florida Coast," and eggs from alligators and various native birds including pelicans and flamingos. Shoppers could even purchase such exotic Florida wonders as "Spanish moss" and "coquina rock" for ten cents to fifty cents each. (One wonders if such rarities could be sold with a straight face.)

Fortunately for Florida's wildlife, the 1890s would see the eccentric curio market eclipsed by more refined and expensive keepsakes. This marked change began with Florida's "Golden Age" around 1890. The arrival of the multimillionaire industrialist Henry Flagler and his subsequent development of St. Augustine and the east coast was a turning point in Florida tourism and Florida souvenirs.

By 1885, Flagler had begun building elegant and expensive hotels for rich New England industrialists with cultivated tastes, and it wasn't long until astute shop owners were offering them sumptuous souvenirs decorated with Florida motifs. Ornate sterling silver, fine European china, and ivory-handled canes joined an array of other exquisite mementos.

Figure 3.3 Postcard of Ranck Souvenir Shop, Rockledge, ca. 1905–1915.

Figure 3.4 G&C, St. Augustine, postcard, ca. 1900–1910.

Businesses such as Greenleaf and Crosby, W. H. DuBois, El Unico, and Osky's offered an incredible array of souvenirs and novelties. Based in Jacksonville, Greenleaf and Crosby maintained shops in all of Flagler's major hotels and was a primary source of Florida souvenirs. Founded in 1867 by Damon Greenleaf, the company soon gained fame as the largest business of its kind, with the best assortment of souvenirs. In 1880, J. H. Crosby Jr. would join the company as a buyer. This ultimately led to a partnership with Greenleaf. By the late 1880s, the company began stocking manufactured goods from New York and imported wares from Europe. The firm also designed and produced its own exquisite line of souvenirs. From its china to its sterling, Greenleaf and Crosby items are prized among today's collectors for quality, detail, and elegant Florida themes.

No less important was Osky's, also in Jacksonville. Founded in 1884, the business focused on "alligator goods," such as purses and luggage, but maintained an excellent variety of Florida souvenirs including china, sterling spoons, canes, and carved alligator items. A number of existing Osky catalogs, dating from ca. 1905–1915, illustrate the variety of souvenirs offered.

The state's increasing popularity as a tourist destination could be attributed to any number of things, from its new luxury hotels to its seductive tropical allure. However, Florida promoters were ambitious, and their guidebooks, promotionals, and exhibitions constantly advanced Florida's "sunny South" appeal.

In 1888, Jacksonville would host the first of four consecutive "Florida Sub Tropical Expositions," held from January to April in conjunction with the winter tourist season. Their primary goal was to promote Florida industry and showcase the state's many and varied assets. Florida souvenirs were well represented, with an exhibit by Damon Greenleaf, the foremost dealer in curiosities in the state. An existing 1888 Sub Tropical Exposition Catalogue offers an extensive list of souvenirs sold at the Greenleaf and Crosby exhibit. A variety of jewelry was for sale, including alligator tooth, fish scale, sea bean, and carved boar tusk jewelry. Even alligator skulls and fans made of native bird feathers were sold.

Florida's greatest promotional venture was its participation in the World's Columbian Exposition of 1893, held in Chicago. The four-hundred-year celebration of Columbus's landing in America, with its Spanish-American connotations, proved the perfect stage for Florida and its hopes for international attention. Using the Exposition's premise, Florida would draw upon its varied history and Spanish heritage in the design of its state pavilion. An ample 1:5 scale replica of Ft. Marion was built to house displays that featured Florida's history as well as its natural resources. Curiosities such as stuffed alligators, orangewood canes, and shell novelties were offered as souvenirs.

Of the forty representative state pavilions, Florida's unique colonial fortress design and its exotic atmosphere made it one of the Exposition's most popular destinations.

The Exposition also had a defining effect on souvenirs. It was the largest exhibition of American industry in the nineteenth century, with an average daily attendance of 172,712.

Earlier fairs and exhibitions had sparked an interest in souvenirs, but the Columbian would make it a national phenomenon. Souvenirs were sold by the millions and provided collectors with a variety of beautiful yet inexpensive

Figure 3.5 Interior of Osky's Curio Store, Jacksonville, postcard, ca. 1905–1910.

keepsakes, many with representations of the various Exposition attractions. This inevitably had a positive effect on Florida's growing souvenir trade.

The state's emergence in the 1890s as the top U.S. tourist destination could not have been timed better. Improved transportation enabled prosperous Americans to visit Florida by the thousands. Tourists poured into the state, buying an array of souvenirs, many of which pictured places they had visited.

In part, souvenirs became travel trophies, obvious mementos of success. Souvenir collecting had become the rage, not only in Florida but in the nation as a whole. Shops selling souvenirs abounded. Advertising marks on Florida view china indicate it was sold everywhere, from jewelry stores to pharmacies,

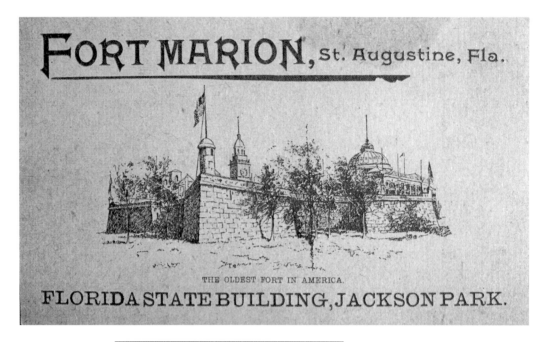

Above: *Figure 3.6 Florida Building Columbian Exposition, 1893, from the business card of E. A. Waddell, a Florida exhibitor from Key West. The back of the card features souvenirs he sold at the Expo, including "sand . . . where Columbus landed," as well as "sea fans, star fish, porcupine fish, swordfish, tortoise-shell turtles, conches, coral, shell work of all kinds."*

Left: *Figure 3.7 Florida Exposition metal souvenir from the Chicago World's Fair, 1893.*

Florida's Golden Age of Souvenirs

FACTORY No. 649   FIRST DIST. N.Y.

ORMOND BEACH

Figure 3.8 Ormond Beach tobacco silk of a Florida bathing beauty, ca. 1900–1910.

from bookstores to toy shops. Even the Palm Beach Bicycle and Electric Co. sold souvenir china bearing the firm's mark.

As we will see in the following chapters, souvenirs were not limited just to popular east coast destinations. Many small-town businesses featured local souvenirs as a part of their stores' running inventories.

By the end of the Golden Age around 1930 and with the Depression of 1930–1941 that followed, there was an appreciable decline in tourism and the novelty trade. Still, the souvenir industry survived by turning from the more refined mementos to the cheaper Japanese imitations, thus establishing the standards for post–World War II souvenirs.

Souvenir China

It is easy to understand the popularity of china souvenirs. Their refined beauty, almost endless variety, and historical significance rank them among Florida's most desirable types of souvenirs.

Fortunately for today's enthusiasts, china mementos were a favorite among Victorian travelers. They were usually small and easily transported. By far the most popular of this genre were the illustrated wares, often referred to as scenic, view, or picture china. The majority were produced in European potteries, noted for their fine ceramic traditions, with German factories dominating until World War I. (America had no ceramic industrial base capable of meeting such intensive production demands.) As a rule, all Florida souvenir china is a form of utilitarian ware and can range from toothpick holders to teapots, with plates being the most popular. It is often marked by the manufacturer, importer, and local distributor, providing a link to its origin and local history.

The American companies that ordered souvenir china would supply postcards, photographs, and the like that would then be copied at the factory by engraving the image on steel or copper plates. From these, sheets of printed transfer decals were made and individually burnished onto the porcelain ware before firing. The transfers were either left as a contrast to the white surface or hand colored by artisans.

The scenes on ceramic souvenirs give us a special and expanded look at old Florida. Forgotten buildings and tranquil street scenes, gone or changed forever, remind us of an innocence lost. Colorful natural views are frequently found on plates, whose form lends them to such settings, their translucent surfaces often illuminated with quiet rivers and sunlit shores, where stately palms stand like silent sentinels.

Figural mementos are another type of souvenir china, one often overlooked by souvenir collectors. Among my favorites are porcelain bathing beauties. These alluring ladies playfully tease the viewer into enjoying a captive moment of seaside fun.

Florida fauna is well represented by its many figural keepsakes, which are often whimsical and animated. As can be expected, alligators, pelicans, and flamingos are the most common, but marine life, such as lobsters, crabs, and even stingrays, can also be found.

Picture china has a colorful history. The first impetus toward reproducing images on china came from the success of cobalt-decorated historical Staffordshire dinnerware manufactured in the early nineteenth century, until about 1860. Produced in Staffordshire, England, the china illustrated patriotic American themes and was quite popular at the time.

The Centennial Exposition in Philadelphia in 1876 would witness the next important step in the development of souvenir china. The Pratt pottery of Fenton, England, produced an exquisite line of colorful plates that exhibited scenes of the various Exposition buildings and were well received.

Next came the Wedgwood cobalt-decorated china of the 1880s. This, no doubt, was a reintroduction of the successful Staffordshire-type wares of the first half of the nineteenth century. Only a limited number of scenes were produced, with only one Florida example known to the author (see fig. 4.113).

The final stage of this chronological review is the Columbian Exposition of 1893, a historic marker for all souvenirs from the Golden Age. Millions of people attended this grand event. Vast quantities of keepsakes were produced for the Exposition and were an instant success. China picturing varied Exposition buildings was well received, including the blue Staffordshire-type tableware. However, English china would, for the first time, come up against keen competition. Germany and Austria would introduce their own line of inexpensive and colorful porcelain souvenirs, successfully securing their future in the souvenir china trade. By 1894, a year after the Columbian Exposition, agents from America began placing orders for hometown views with German and Austrian potteries. Soon these two countries would dominate the U.S. markets.

Many wholesale companies sold Florida view china but most limited their production to well-known tourist destinations, such as St. Augustine or Jacksonville. Still, two companies, C. E. Wheelock and John H. Roth, stand out in their efforts to market their wares throughout the state. Ultimately all of Florida's major cities and most smaller towns would be represented on one form of china or another. Because of the widespread efforts of these two firms, the majority of remaining souvenir china that exists today is from one company or the other. Both businesses imported their china from Germany and Austria until World War I, when they turned to England to supplement their trade.

What follows is a quick historical synopsis of Wheelock, Jonroth, and other known distributors of Florida scenic china.

1. C. E. Wheelock and Company, Peoria, Illinois, 1888–1971
The Wheelock Company became a serious importer of view china in 1894 after company representatives witnessed its success at the Columbian Exposition. Although it does not occur in Florida as frequently as Jonroth, it is highly regarded among collectors for its distinct colorful images and fine artisanship.

When World War I ended imports from Germany, the company turned to England for its souvenir china. These were generally eight-inch blue plates, sometimes called flo-blue because of the tendency for the cobalt design to fade or flow into the background. These usually had five or six views of equal size placed around the plate, with one scene in the middle (see fig. 4.133). Most are marked "England" and date between 1916 and 1922. After World War I, Wheelock's interest in souvenir china waned, and the company eventually discontinued production.

2. John Roth and Company, Peoria, Illinois, 1909–present
Roth was employed by the Wheelock Company for twenty-one years. By 1909 he had left to begin his own business in Peoria, Illinois, directly competing with Wheelock. Of the two importers, Roth captured most of the Florida market. His palette mark, the initials J. H. R., or condensed name, "Jonroth," appears on 65 percent of the eight-seven importer-marked examples in my own collection.

Roth established the market for colorful full-face plate plaques, where the view covers the entire surface of the form (see fig. 4.52). They range in size from four inches to eight inches and are unique to the John Roth Company. Roth introduced the full-picture plates shortly after opening his business in 1909 and continued manufacturing them until the early 1930s. With the advent of World War I, Roth, like Wheelock, had to turn to English manufacturers, and he began to concentrate on developing the market for his Staffordshire cobalt blue multiview china. After the war he was able to partially restore his import ties with Germany, thus securing his postwar dominance of the trade.

The company is still owned by the Roth family, now in its third generation, and is the longest-running business of its kind. John H. Roth III lives in and operates the company out of Florida.

The souvenir china listed next was all made in England and was decorated with blue-and-white transfer scenes. All were plate plaques, popular at the time.

3. Rowland and Marsellus, New York, 1893–1937
Most of the R and M souvenir china was made between ca. 1900 and ca. 1915 and was known for its rich cobalt blue color. Although R and M produced tableware, such as tumblers, cups and saucers, and the like, all known view china from

Florida was produced on plates. Some of these were the peculiar rolled-edge type (see fig. 4.91). The edges of these plates have six cameo scenes with a central view and measure ten inches in diameter.

4. Bawo and Dotter, New York, 1864–1910
Bawo and Dotter produced ware very similar to that of Rowland and Marsellus, importing some with identical decorations. In certain cases, the manufacturer's mark on the bottom of the plate is the only way to tell one from the other (see fig. 4.90).

Figure 4.1 Spanish American War 1898, depicting Uncle Sam and a Spanish matador standing on a tobacco leaf and pulling at a large cigar mkd. "Cuba," represents Spain's ban on Cuban tobacco sales to the United States in 1896. The embargo was aimed at Cuban cigar makers in Key West and Tampa who generously supported Cuban revolutionaries in their fight against Spanish rule and sent them arms and munitions. The ban on tobacco added to America's growing antagonism toward Spain, which ultimately led to the Spanish American War of 1898.

Figure 4.2 Whiskey jug, 8", featuring Johnny Griffin (see figure 5.44). G&C cat., ca. 1900–1910.

Figure 4.3 Alligator toothpick holders, ca. 1900–1910, both 3 ¼".

Figure 4.4 Porcelain bathing beauties in a number of different styles were particularly popular during the Roaring Twenties. 1 ½" to 3 ½".

Figure 4.5 Orangeware souvenirs, which usually depict marine animals, figural oranges, and serving pieces. The fish and two crabs are trinket boxes; the stingray is a pin tray. Each 3"–4", ca. 1900–1910.

Figure 4.6 Three orangeware lobsters; l to r, box 3½" long mkd. "Tampa"; creamer 3" h. mkd. "Florida"; pintray 4" long mkd. "Florida."

Figure 4.7 Orangeware creamer and sugar with applied alligator and orange blossom decorations, ca. 1890–1900. Both 3", stenciled in gold "From Florida."

Figure 4.8 Orangeware cup 2" and saucer 4¼", teapot 5", creamer 3½", ca. 1890–1900. All have applied orange blossoms and leaves and are stenciled in gold "From Florida."

Figure 4.9 Orangeware souvenirs: ct, eggcup; c, S & P; far l and r, pintrays; f, creamer and two miniature sugars. All 2" to 3", mkd. "Florida."

Figure 4.10 St. Augustine, Old City Gateway, figural bisque S & P, 3½" x 4".

Figure 4.11 Figural pig souvenir mkd. "Pensacola" in gold, ca. 1880–1890, 4". One of a genre of souvenirs portraying pigs in a variety of carefree activities, with pigs usually pink and props green.

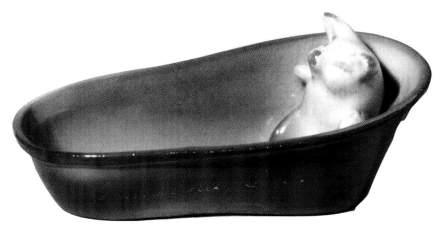

Figure 4.12 Figural alligators S & P with jelly container mkd. "Japan," ca. 1920–1930.

Figure 4.13 St. Augustine tiles, ca. 1880–1890, l, Catholic parish church; r, Old City Gates, both 6″ x 6″.

Figure 4.14 Exquisite tea service sold by G&C features one of several orange patterns the company used on their finer china. Mkd. "Greenleaf & Crosby, Limoges France," made from ca. 1890 until WWI. Teapot 10″, serving tray 12½″ d., cup 3″, saucers 4¾″ d.

Figure 4.15 *One of the orange patterns used by G&C, mkd. "Greenleaf & Crosby Limoges France," made from ca. 1890 until WWI. Larger bowl 11½" d., smaller bowl 9½" d., creamer 4½" h., sugar 4" h.*

Figure 4.16 *Extraordinary set of G&C china illustrating one of the company's superior orange blossom designs mkd. "Greenleaf & Crosby, Limoges France," made from ca. 1890 until WWI. Large pitcher 15½" h., small pitcher 9" h., platter 12½" d.*

Figure 4.17 *Orange bordered plate, 10", reflects a variation of the many decorative designs on Florida china that use oranges and orange blossoms. Sold by "Kings of Jacksonville, Fla.," ca. 1890–1900.*

Figure 4.18 Unique creamer, 4½″, with hand-painted image of the Royal Poinciana Hotel, possibly a winter guest's artistic tribute to their place of residence; china painting was popular at the turn of the century. "The Royal Poinciana Hotel, Palm Beach" is painted on the bottom, ca. 1910–1920.

Figure 4.19 Wedgwood-like jasperware souvenirs, both mkd. "Old City Gates, St. Augustine, Fla." Pitcher 3 ¼″, box 1 ¾″ x 3½″. Though jasperware is usually associated with English potteries, these examples were made in Germany, ca. 1900–1910.

Figure 4.20 Wedgwood-like jasperware ashtrays, both mkd. "Japan," ca. 1920–1930: t, 5″ x 3⅜″; b, 5½″ x 3½″.

Left: *Figure 4.21 Rare St. Augustine delftware pitcher mkd. "Made in Germany" for "A. J. Kolb," 3 ⅝." Kolb is listed in a 1904 St. Augustine directory as selling stationary but must have carried souvenirs as well.*

Below: *Figure 4.22 Jonroth multiview plates, all 6": t, "New Port Richey" scenes, clockwise, "Up the Cotee River, Home of Thomas Meighan, Orange Lake, Hotel Hacienda and Miniature Golf Course"; bl, "Sebring" scenes, clockwise, "Kenilworth Lodge, The Circle, Municipal Pier, Lake Jackson"; br, "Sarasota" scenes, clockwise, "Sarasota County House, Inner Court, Ringling Museum, Mira Mar Hotel Sarasota Bay."*

Bottom: *Figure 4.23 Jonroth multiview plates, all 6": l, "Hollywood" scenes, clockwise, "Hollywood Hotel, on the Beach, Golf and Country Club, Coconut Palm, Hollywood Beach Casino"; r, "Palm Beach" scenes, clockwise, "Royal Poinciana Hotel Entrance to Whitehall, The Alba, The Breakers."*

Florida's Golden Age of Souvenirs

Above: *Figure 4.24 "St. Augustine, Fla." in silver over-lay, "Made by Lenox" of Trenton, N.J., ca. 1910–1920, 2¼", rare example of souvenir china produced in America.*

Right: *Figure 4.25 Jacksonville mug, "Souvenir of the Ostrich Farm," made of majolica, an earthenware pottery popular during the Victorian era, ca. 1890–1900, 2½".*

Below: *Figure 4.26 Ormond tray, "Hotel Ormond, Florida," majolica, with hotel image impressed into the clay surface and overglazed, ca. 1890–1900, 6¼" x 8¾".*

Right: *Figure 4.27 Daytona, "Hotel Clarendon, Daytona Florida," small dish with added pine needle and sweetgrass border commonly associated with Seminole Indian basketmakers, 7¼" including pine needle addition, ca. 1910–1920.*

Below: *Figure 4.28 Mettlach tumblers, views, l, St. Augustine, l to r, "Old City Gates, Old Watch Tower, Old Slave Market"; c, Palm Beach, l to r, "Morning Sidewalk. Hotel Royal Poinciana. Ocean Avenue"; r, St. Augustine, color variation on view l.*

Bottom: *Figure 4.29 St. Augustine steins, l, typical German-made stein, 7¾"; r, stein made by Whites Pottery Co., Utica, N.Y., cobalt-decorated stoneware, ca. 1890–1900, 4¾".*

Florida's Golden Age of Souvenirs

Left: *Figure 4.30 St. Augustine German Mettlach steins, views, l to r, "Fort Marion, Spanish Coat of Arms, Old City Gates," ca. 1890–1910. L, 7½"; r, 8½", both sold by G&C.*

Below: *Figure 4.31 Porcelain steins, l to r, "Florida State College, Tallahassee, Fla.," 3¾"; "Beautiful Springfield the Waterworks, Jacksonville, Fla" made for "J. Osky, Jacksonville Fla," 5¾"; "U. S. Customs House, Post Office & American National Bank, Pensacola Fla.," made for "Will O. Diffenderfer," 6½"; "Riverside Park, Jacksonville, Fla" made for "J. Osky," 5¾".*

Bottom: *Figure 4.32 Stoneware steins, turn of the century, l to r: "The Royal Poinciana Hotel, Palm Beach Fla.," 4¾"; "Souvenir of Jacksonville, Fla," l side, "Hotel Seminole," r side, "Windsor Hotel," 4½"; "Jacksonville, Fla., Hotel Mason," 7"; "Souvenir of Jacksonville," l, "Hotel Seminole," r, "Windsor Hotel," 7"; "Souvenir of Jacksonville, Hotel Windsor," l, "Post Office," r, "Confederate Monument," 7"; "Jacksonville, Fla," "Hotel Seminole," 4".*

Above: *Figure 4.33 German figural steins, l to r, made by Bohn Söhne, 6″; mkd. "Musterschutz," G&C cat., ca. 1900–1910, 7″; mkd. "Marzi & Remy 1914," 6″.*

Right: *Figure 4.34 Steins from Hampshire pottery, Keene, N.H., 1871–1923, one of the few American ceramic companies that produced a line of souvenirs; Florida examples are extremely rare. Both mkd. "Ladies Parlor, Silver Springs, Fla.," ca. 1900–1910.*

Below: *Figure 4.35 St. Augustine steins, l to r, views, l to r, "City Gates, Ft. Marion and Spanish Crest," 8½″; "Ft. Marion Water Battery, Spanish Crest, Old City Gate," 6¼″; "Old City Gates, St. Augustine, Fla" mkd. "W. H. Duboise El Unico St. Augustine," 5″.*

Above: *Figure 4.36 Florida steins,* l to r, *views,* l to r, *"Souvenir of Florida,"* alligator, Spanish crest, banjo player, 4½" and 8"; *"Souvenir of Florida,"* 8"; alligator, Spanish crest, and alligator on orange, 7".

Left: *Figure 4.37 Florida mugs,* l to r, *"The Breakers, Palm Beach Fla.,"* 3⅛"; *"Ostrich Farm, Driving Ostrich, Jacksonville, Fla."* sold by *"Osky's,"* 4½"; *"Kingsley Lake, Starke, Fla.,"* 2¾".

Below: *Figure 4.38 Arcadia dish,* *"Desoto County Orange Grove,"* made for *"F. Marqus,"* 5½".

Above: *Figure 4.39 Bradenton water pail, "Manatee River Bridge," 4".*

Below: *Figure 4.40 Bradenton celery dish, "Manatee River From Braidentown, Fla." made for "Braidentown Hardware Co.," 4⅛" x 9".*

Right: *Figure 4.41 Branford platter, "A Bridge Over The Suwannee," 10"; urn 11½", four cups 2½" to 3"; saucers 5". All titled "The Suwanee River" made for "Horn & Key."*

Above: *Figure 4.42 Clearwater creamer 2¾"; fold-corner dish 4⅛", both mkd. "Peace Memorial Presbyterian Church" and made for "Russell M. Martin."*

Left: *Figure 4.43 Crescent City dish, "Grove Hall Crescent City, Fla." made for "C. H. Preston Co."*

Below: *Figure 4.44 Crystal River dish, "Dixon Cedar Mill" made for "Crystal River Drug Co.," 6".*

Top: *Figure 4.45 Daytona jar 3″; vase 4″, both "Beach Street Looking N."*

Above: *Figure 4.46 Daytona celery dish, views, l to r, "Along the Halifax River," "Cedar Street," "Volusia Avenue and Three branched Palmetto," 4½″ x 12⅛″.*

Left: *Figure 4.47 Daytona plate, "Souvenir of Daytona" sold by "J. L. Wallace," 8″.*

Above: *Figure 4.48 Daytona plate, "Ridgewood Hotel" made for "M. A. Justin," 8".*

Right: *Figure 4.49 Daytona multiview plate, clockwise, "The Grand Canal, by Santa Lucia Island, Elk's Club, Clarendon Hotel, Royal Arch Oak," 8½".*

Below: *Figure 4.50 DeFuniak Springs dish, "Hotel Chautauqua," 5".*

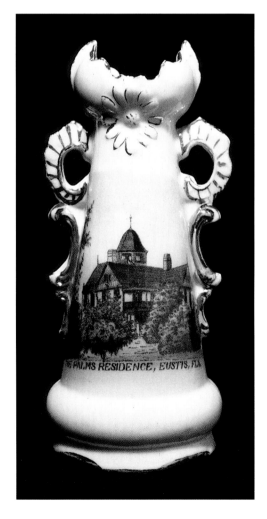

Figure 4.51 Deland creamer and sugar, l, "Elizabeth Hall, Stetson University"; r, "President's Residence Stetson University," both about 2½" h. x 4", scenes highlighted in gold.

Figure 4.52 Delray dish, "Gulf Stream Golf Club, Delray, Fla." made for "L. M. Miles," 4¾".

Figure 4.53 Eustis vase, "The Palms Residence," 4¾".

Above: *Figure 4.54 Eustis plate, "Three Graces," 8½".*

Right: *Figure 4.55 Eustis chocolate pot, "Lake Eustis," 10".*

Below: *Figure 4.56 Fernandina disaster cup and saucer: cup, "Nassau County Court House"; saucer, "Foot of Center Street, After Storm Oct. 2, 1898," 5½" d., made for "P. R. Brady."*

Above: *Figure 4.57 Ft. Lauderdale plate, "Seminole Indian Camp, Ft. Lauderdale Fla." made for "The Post Card Shop," 6¼".*

Right: *Figure 4.58 Ft. Lauderdale dish, "Home of the Seminole, Pine Island, Fla." sold by "Barryhill-Cromartis Co.," 5½".*

Below: *Figure 4.59 Ft. Meade plate, "Public School Building," 7".*

Above: *Figure 4.60 Ft. Myers creamer, "Royal Palm Hotel," 2½".*

Right: *Figure 4.61 Ft. Myers plate, "Tarpon or Silver King Caught at Myers, Fla." made for "W. R. Washburn," 7¼".*

Below: *Figure 4.62 Ft. Pierce plate, "The Store" made for "P. P. Cobb," 6½".*

Above: *Figure 4.63 Gainesville vase, "Alachua County Court House, Gainesville, Fla.," 3¼"; fold-corner dish, "Public School Gainesville, Fla." made for "Miller & Avera," 4⅛"; cup, "Court House, Gainesville, Fla.," 2¾".*

Right: *Figure 4.64 Gainesville cobalt blue multiview plate, clockwise, "First Baptist Church, Holy Trinity Episcopal Church, Roman Catholic Church, Methodist Episcopal Church South, Church of Christ,"; c, "Advent Christian Church." Made in England for "Saunders Grocery Co.," ca. 1915–1925, 7¾".*

Below: *Figure 4.65 Green Cove Springs cup, "Rapid Transit," 3⅛".*

Florida's Golden Age of Souvenirs

Above: *Figure 4.66 Jacksonville plate, "Bay Street, East of Laura" made for "J. Osky," 7".*

Right: *Figure 4.67 Jacksonville multiview plate, clockwise, "Main Street, City Hall, Hotel Windsor, Hemming Park" made for "J. Osky," 7".*

Below: *Figure 4.68 Jacksonville matching tumblers, color variations. Views, l to r, "Duval County Court House, Windsor Hotel, Bay Street," 3 ¾".*

Figure 4.69 Jacksonville plate, "Scene on the St. Johns River" made for "T. C. Imeson," 8½".

Figure 4.70 Jacksonville plate, "Windsor Hotel" made for "Women's Exchange," 7".

Figure 4.71 Jacksonville multiview plate, clockwise, "Hemming Park and Windsor Hotel, Hotel Seminole, St. John's River, Post Office" made for "Thos. C. Imeson," 8".

Left: *Figure 4.72 Jacksonville plate, "Moonlight on the St. Johns River" made for "Jacksonville Photo Supply, Inc.," 6".*

Below: *Figure 4.73 Jacksonville urn and creamer, both mkd. "Jacksonville Florida," 2¾" and 3½"; metal gator, 3". Alligators playing musical instruments were fairly common motifs, especially for metal souvenirs.*

Bottom: *Figure 4.74 Jacksonville plate, "Hemming Park, Jacksonville, Florida" made for "A. S. Levi," 7".*

Above: *Figure 4.75 Jacksonville creamers, l, "Bay Street, One Year After the Fire," ca. 1902, 4"; r, "Windsor Hotel and Park," 2 ¾".*

Right: *Figure 4.76 Jacksonville multiview plate, clockwise, "Windsor Hotel, Court House, Elks Club, Hemming Park, Library and First Presbyterian Church, Post Office, Government Building," 7".*

Below: *Figure 4.77 Jacksonville plate, "After Great Fire, May 3rd, 1901" made for "R. I. Riles," 7".*

Above: *Figure 4.78 Jacksonville rolled-edge plate, c,* "Government and Post Office Building"; *rim,* clockwise, "Windsor Hotel, City Gates, St. Augustine, St. John's River *and Bridge, Hemming Park, City Hall." Imported by "Bawo and Dotter" for the "Knight Crockery and Furniture Co.," 10".*

Right: *Figure 4.79 Key West plate, "Hotel Casa Marina, South Shore," 8¼".*

Below: *Figure 4.80 Key West creamer, "Long Key Viaduct 2.4 Miles Long and First Passenger Train to Knight Key," 3" d. x 3½" h.*

Above: *Figure 4.81 Lake Helen candy dish, "Harlan in the Pines," 5 ¾" x 7 ¼".*

Left: *Figure 4.82 Lakeland tumbler, "Lakeland High School" made for "Lakeland Bookstore," 3 ⅞".*

Below: *Figure 4.83 Lake Wales plate, "Bok Singing Tower, Mountain Lake" made for "Cindy's Gift and Art Shop," 8". Bok Tower opened as a tourist attraction in 1929.*

Top: *Figure 4.84 Live Oak plate, "Howard Street, Looking West" made for "Florida Book & News Co.," 7½".*

Above: *Figure 4.85 Live Oak creamer, "General Store Building, M. L. Burnett 203 and 206 West Howard St." made for "M. L. Burnett," 3⅜".*

Right: *Figure 4.86 Melbourne pintray, "New Haven Ave. Melbourne," 3 ¼" x 4⅜"; dish, "The Hotel Melbourne," 4".*

Above: *Figure 4.87 Miami plate, "Royal Palm Hotel and Grounds" made for "Buena Vista Dept. Store," 8½".*

Right: *Figure 4.88 Miami tumbler, "Biscayne Drive," 3¾".*

Below: *Figure 4.89 Miami creamer, "Halcyon Hall," 2½"; pail, "Avenue of Royal Palms, Musa Isle Grove," 3".*

Top: *Figure 4.90 Miami rolled-edge plate, c,
"Cape Florida Lighthouse"; rim scenes,* clock-
wise, *"Seminole Club and Giant Bamboos,
Royal Palm Hotel, Entrance to Fort Dallas
Park, Old Fort Dallas, Coconut Trees 12th St.
and Boulevard, Halcyon Hall and Avenue B,"
imported by Bawo and Dotter for "H. T.
Whaler."*

Above: *Figure 4.91 Miami cobalt blue rolled-
edge plate, c, "Chief Osceola"; rim scenes,
clockwise, "Hotel Royal Palm, Old Fort Dallas, Mouth of Miami River, Halcyon Hall,
The Road to Coconut Grove, Steamship Miami," imported by "Rowland and Marsellus"
for G&C.*

Left: *Figure 4.92 Mosquito Inlet bowl, "Mosquito Inlet Light, Seacoast of Florida," 2½" h.,
5¾" d. Lighthouse on the Halifax River at
Ponce Inlet just south of Daytona.*

Figure 4.93 Mulberry dish, "Prairie Pebble Phosphate Co. Polk County, Fla." made for "McRillop & Swearingen," 5 ¾".

Figure 4.94 New Smyrna creamer, "Hillsboro Street," 2 ¾"; cup, "Ruins of the Old Spanish Mission," 2 ¾".

Figure 4.95 Orlando vase, "Watkins Block Corner Pine and Orange Avenue," 2 ⅞"; creamer, same title, 2 ¾".

Figure 4.96 Palatka bowl, "Devil's Elbow, St. John's River" made for "F. A. Gerber & Son," 2⅛"; creamer, "The City Hall," 3 ¾".

Figure 4.97 Palatka spooner, "Putnam House" made for "Capt. M. R. Ryan," 4¼".

Figure 4.98 "Putnam House" postcard.

Figure 4.99 Palm Beach plate, "The Breakers" made for "Dixie Souvenir Shop, 6⅛".

Figure 4.100 Palm Beach cobalt blue plate, c, "Royal Poinciana, Palm Beach Florida"; rim scenes, clockwise, "Morningside Walk, Lake Front, Main Entrance Royal Poinciana, Royal Palm, Jungle, The Breakers," imported by Rowland and Marcellas.

Figure 4.101 Pensacola dish, "New L & N Depot" made for "Mrs. L. J. McClure," 5⅞".

Figure 4.102 Pensacola sugar, "Tarragona Street, Wharf & City Hall," 4⅛"; creamer, "The Plaza Fountain," 4¼," both made for "Will O. Diffenderfer."

Figure 4.103 Pensacola plate, "Looking North on Palafox Street" made for "Palace Jewelry Co.," 7⅜".

Figure 4.104 Pensacola plate, "Mammie, Pensacola, Fla." made for "Peter Lindenstruth," 7¾".

Figure 4.105 Sanford creamer, "Sanford House" made for "A. E. Hill," 3 ¾".

Figure 4.106 Sanford box, "Sanford House Park," 2 ⅛" h., 3 ¼" d.

Figure 4.107 Sarasota plate, "Women's Club" made for "Sarasota Art Shop," 6 ⅛".

Figure 4.108 Sebring plate, "Lake Jackson at Center Avenue," 6¼".

Figure 4.109 Sebring plate, "Kenilworth Lodge, Sebring, Fla.," 6½".

Figure 4.110 Silver Springs plate, "Glass Bottom Boats at Silver Springs, Fla.," 6⅝".

Figure 4.111 Silver Springs celery dish, "The Famous Silver Springs, Six Miles From Ocala, Fla." made for "Anti Monopoly Drugstore, Ocala, Fla.," 2¾" x 9¼".

Figure 4.112 Starke plate, "Clay Street," 7⅝".

Figure 4.113 St. Augustine plate, "City Gates St. Augustine, Fla.," 10", ca. 1880–1890.

Figure 4.114 St. Augustine plate, "Old City Gates," made in "Limoges, France," sold by G&C, 8¼".

Figure 4.115 St. Augustine plate, Spanish crest, 8"; pitcher, Spanish crest, 7", both made for "W. H. DuBois."

Figure 4.116 St. Augustine teapot, f, "Ponce de Leon Hotel," b, "Slave Market" made for "R. B. Allen," 7½".

Figure 4.117 St. Augustine plate, "Fort Marion Showing Water Battery and Hot Shot Oven" made for "J. E. Snider Co.," 7".

Figure 4.118 St. Augustine cup, 2 ¼", and saucer 4", orange decoration, made for "King's" of St. Augustine.

Figure 4.119 St. Augustine plates, l, Columbus plate made for the "Casa Monica Hotel," opened in 1888 and purchased by Flagler in 1889, becoming the "Cordova"; r, "To Castille and Leon was given a New World, San Salvador A.D. 1492," G&C cat., ca. 1900–1910.

Figure 4.120 St. Augustine plate, orange blossom and Spanish crest, 7½".

Figure 4.121 St. Augustine, two creamers, l, "Oldest House in U. S.," 3⅛"; r, "Hotel Ponce de Leon," 3½", both made for "Usina Bros."

Figure 4.122 St. Augustine basketweave dishes, l, "Fort Marion," 5" d.; r, "Old City Gates," 3" d.

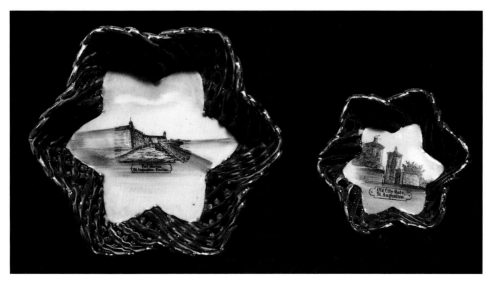

Figure 4.123 St. Augustine plate, "Fort Marion," 7".

Figure 4.124 St. Augustine plate, "City Gates" with fancy orange blossom borders, 9½".

Figure 4.125 St. Augustine dishes: palate-shaped dish, "Memorial Church St. Augustine," 5½"; fold-corner dish, "Ponce de Leon Hotel," 4¼".

Figure 4.126 St. Augustine plate, Spanish coat of arms, orange blossom border, 8½".

Figure 4.127 St. Augustine plates, both mkd. "Landing of Juan Ponce de Leon, St. Augustine, Florida March 24th 1512." Plate on r, in G&C cat., ca. 1900–1910, l, 8⅛"; r, 8".

Figure 4.128 St. Augustine cup, "Old City Gates," 2½"; saucer, "Hotel Cordova," "Old Cathedral," 5½"; plates, "Old City Gates," "Juan Ponce de Leon Florida March 27th 1512," both 9¾". All G&C cat., ca. 1900–1910.

Figure 4.129 St. Petersburg vase, "High School Building," 3 ⅛"; wall pocket, "Central Avenue," 4½"; hat, "The Shell Fence," 2¼".

Figure 4.130 St. Petersburg candy dish, "Detroit Hotel," 4¾" x 7½".

Figure 4.131 Sutherland plate, "Girls' Dormitory Florida Seminary, Sutherland, Fla." made for "N. F. McDonald, Sutherland, Fla.," 7".

Figure 4.132 *Tallahassee plate, "State Capitol" made for "Mrs. Fitzgerald's Gift Shop," 7".*

Figure 4.133 *Tallahassee multiview plate, scenes, c, "State College for Women"; clockwise, "Governor's Mansion, Government Buildings & Park, Bryan Hall, East Hall, State Capitol" made for "Gilmore & Davis Co.," 7¾".*

Figure 4.134 *Tallahassee plate, "Florida State College for Women" made for "Mrs. Fitzgerald's Gift Shop," 7".*

Figure 4.135 Tarpon Springs plate, "Tarpon Springs The Venice of the South" made for "N. Gamse."

Figure 4.136 Tarpon Springs vases, l, "Sponge Diver," 5½"; r, "Sponge Exchange," 7¼", both made for "Jack's Curio Store."

Figure 4.137 Tampa fold-corner dish, "Tampa Bay Hotel," 4¾".

Figure 4.138 Tampa cups and saucers, l, "Tampa Bay Hotel"; tc, "Tampa Bay Hotel"; bc, "Post Office"; r, "Post Office." Cups 2½", saucers 4¾", all made for "M. Ressler."

Figure 4.139 Tampa multiview plate, clockwise, "City Hall, Post Office and Court House, Tampa Bay Hotel" made for "M. Ressler."

Figure 4.140 Tampa dish, "Post Office and Custom House" made for "The Shaw Clayton Stationary Co.," 5½"; plate, "German American Club" made for "Dombrosky Jewelry Co.," 6¾".

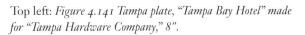

Top left: *Figure 4.141 Tampa plate, "Tampa Bay Hotel" made for "Tampa Hardware Company," 8".*

Top right: *Figure 4.142 Tampa vase, "From Franklin Street Looking South," 6".*

Right: *Figure 4.143 Tampa plate, "Tampa Bay Hotel" made for "J. W. Eckart," 6 ¼".*

Above: *Figure 4.144 Tampa rolled-edge plate, "Tampa Bay Hotel," rim border scenes,* clockwise, *"Customs House and Post Office, Tampa, Fla., Cigar Factory Tampa, Fla., The Belleview Belleair, Fla., Pass-A-Grille Fla. in January, Fishing at St. Petersburg, Fla., Citizen's Bank and Trust Co. Tampa, Fla.," blurred mark, imported by "Rowland and Marsellus."*

Souvenir Spoons

During the Victorian era, sterling silver spoons enjoyed universal appeal among the well-traveled upper class and were regarded as the select souvenir of fashion. What better memento than a beautiful objet d'art depicting detailed views of a day remembered?

Spoons, like scenic china, were enthusiastically embraced during the Golden Age and were equally as popular. Travelers began buying spoons wherever they went, as incidental purchases became full-blown collections. Unlike imported scenic china, the majority of souvenir spoons were made in America. Most came from New England manufacturers, who were quick to grasp the trend. By the 1890s, tourists would have thousands of exquisite spoons to select from.

As with scenic china, the Columbian Exposition of 1893 fueled the passion for souvenir spoons, with more than five hundred produced for this exhibition alone.

Florida's rapidly growing tourist trade ensured a ready market for souvenir spoons. Spoon manufacturers rose to the call and produced an array of beautifully detailed designs. Some of the bowls and handles reflected Florida's defining mix of history, natural beauty, and exotic wildlife. Others focused on the state's development, with detailed renderings of new government buildings, grand hotels, and public parks. No attraction went unnoticed as souvenir spoons captured Florida's charms and achievements in vivid detail.

To appreciate the spoons' artistic merits we need to understand the basic manufacturing techniques and applied decorative methods used. The following information should help clarify most of the initial questions a collector might have.

Manufacturing

1. Die-stamped spoons (see fig. 5.41)
Most souvenir spoons produced for the Florida market were die stamped, a process similar to minting coins. This was achieved by crafting the desired image, in reverse, into a steel block, the die. The more malleable silver was then forced under immense pressure into the harder die. If both sides were to be decorated, double dies were used. Die stamping is a relatively simple and cost effective process.
2. Cast spoons
Essentially, casting involves forming the designed spoon out of wax. The wax model is then placed in liquid plaster. When the plaster has hardened, it is heated to liquefy the wax preform, which is poured from the mold. The remaining spoon-shaped cavity is then filled with liquid silver. When the silver cools, the mold is opened and the spoon removed. Because the process was time consuming and used more silver than did die stamping, Florida examples are rare.
3. Constructed Spoons (see figs. 5.42 and 5.55)
Constructed spoons were not wholly manufactured, that is, they were in some way assembled by craftsmen. Two types are of note. First, handmade spoons were probably made by skilled local jewelers, who used alligator teeth to accentuate the handles. In my ten years of looking for Florida spoons, I have seen only three examples. Their rarity may suggest they were specially made as gifts or possibly as presentation pieces.

The second type of constructed spoon involves silver soldering small premade embellishments to the spoon handles or bowls. These fanciful decorations often included various kinds of sea life. Also popular were applied medallions of Florida's state seal or the Spanish coat of arms (see fig. 5.31).

Decoration

Understanding how the spoons were made is a good foundation. Next, we turn to decoration. For the most part, there were six approaches to bowl and handle ornamentation. Sometimes they were used singly, sometimes in combination with one another.

1. Die stamp (see fig. 5.51)
In die stamping, as explained for spoon manufacture, the motifs are cut into a steel die block, then formed under extreme pressure, leaving an embossed or relief image on the spoon. This was by far the most common form of Florida souvenir spoon decoration.
2. Die cut (see fig. 5.39)
Die cutting was used on handles to remove sections of the silver, creating a negative space and the resulting design. A special cutout die stamp was used to create

this effect. These spoons commonly date between 1915 and 1925.

3. Engraved (see fig. 5.29)

Engraved spoons were more expensive than die-stamped spoons because there was added labor involved in their manufacture. To engrave a spoon, the desired picture is drawn or transferred to the bowl's surface. At this point, a craftsperson carefully incises the rendering with a steel graving tool, cutting the heavier defining lines first and then completing the detail of the picture with finer finishing cuts. The lettering, the final task, is usually cut on the outside edge of the spoon, just above or below the completed picture. Occasionally, handles are engraved with a name, date, or initial. These spoons were usually engraved by local jewelers.

4. Enamel

Because of their refined beauty, enameled spoons are highly prized among current spoon collectors, or "spooners." Their polychrome handles and bowls add a colorful dimension to an otherwise monochromatic silver collection.

Enameling involves the use of finely powdered opaque glass that is mixed in a liquid medium. The individual colors are applied to an existing design and then heated to liquefy the enamel and bind it to the silver. After the spoon has cooled, the resulting image is coated with a protective clear enamel glaze and fired once again.

The following descriptions apply to the four types of enameling used on Florida souvenir spoons.

a. Painted enamel (see fig. 5.18r)

As the name implies, painted enamel spoons were actually hand painted with select enamel colors. Once the picture was painted, the spoon went through the aforementioned firings to complete the overglaze process.

b. Enameled transfer (see fig. 5.1)

Essentially, enameled transfer involves applying a black enamel transferred image to the spoon bowl or handle. This in turn is fired to secure it to the silver. The resulting picture is then painted with the desired colored enamels and fired once again. Finally, a clear enamel is brushed over the picture and the result is fired once more.

c. Champlevé (see fig. 5.19)

The champlevé technique was quite simple. When the die stamp was made, a specified design on the mold was pressed into the silver to create an outline of the desired image. Then the existing shallow recesses between the indentations were filled with the required enamel colors, and the spoon was fired again. This process is often confused with cloisonné, a more costly and complicated procedure.

d. Embossed enameling (see fig. 5.23)

Embossed enameling is the simplest approach to enameling spoons. Spaces between the raised designs on die-stamped spoons are simply filled with the individual enamel colors, and the spoon heated as previously described.

5. Acid etching (see fig. 5.26)

To prepare the spoon for acid etching, the surface to be etched is coated with a white colorant. Then the desired image is transferred to the treated surface. A scribe is used to trace the lines of the design onto the silver. The colorant is then removed and the intended negative areas are coated with an acid-resistant fixative such as resin or aspaltum. Finally the design is covered with an acid wash, which slowly dissolves the exposed silver until the desired image has been achieved.

Acid etching appears to be one of the earlier forms of decoration used on Florida spoons, usually appearing on silver patterns between c. 1895 and 1905.
6. Gold washing or electroplating (see fig. 5.6)
The term "gold wash" refers to a coloring process called electroplating. To achieve the desired gilt, the spoon's handle or bowl is dipped into an electrically charged bath containing trace elements of gold. Through electrolysis, the charged gold bonds with the silver, leaving a thin "gold-washed" field. This gives a handsome contrast to the silver.

Understanding the souvenir spoons' historical and technical aspects helps explain their special appeal. The following pages illustrate the remarkable variety of delicate designs used to change a simple utilitarian utensil into a work of art.

Figure 5.1 Palm Beach, "The Breakers, Palm Beach, Fla." Enm. transfer bowl illustrates beauty and detail typical of such spoons.

Figure 5.2 Jacksonville, "Oliver W. Jr., Jacksonville, Fla.," enm. transfer bowl. Oliver was a popular ride and attraction among tourists visiting the Florida Ostrich Farm, opened 1891.

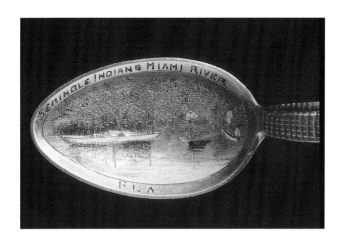

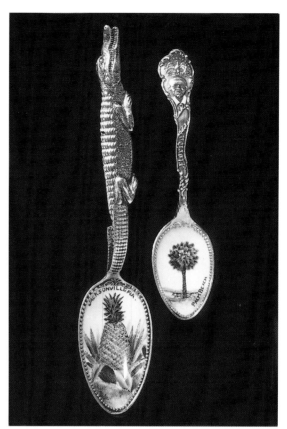

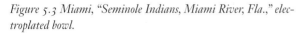

Figure 5.3 Miami, "Seminole Indians, Miami River, Fla.," electroplated bowl.

Figure 5.4 "Jacksonville, Fla.," pineapple, enm. bowl with full-figure alligator han., "Palm Beach" palm tree on bottom, enm. bowl, 5 o'clock size. Black boy tip with enm. collar.

Figure 5.5 Spanish crest enm. bowls, "Jacksonville, Fla." eng. bowl; 5 o'clock size, full crest bowl. Popular motif usually associated with St. Augustine often appears on spoons from other towns.

Figure 5.6 Sugar server, Spanish crest, enm., gold-washed bowl, 4¼".

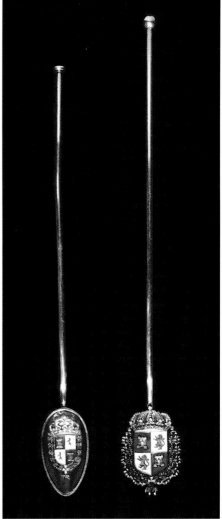

Figure 5.7 *Spanish crests, full enm. bowl, "bonbons."*

Figure 5.8 *St. Augustine, Spanish crest "tea sips," enm. bowls. Spoon han.
are long slender tubes for sipping tea.*

Figure 5.9 *St. Augustine, Spanish crest, enm. bowl.*

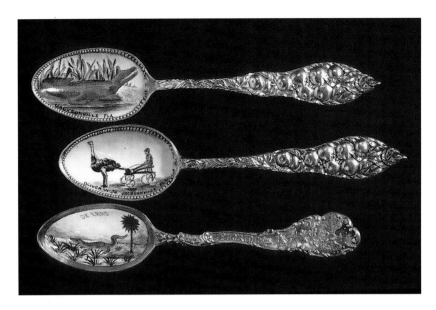

*Figure 5.10 Enm. bowl spoons, l to r, "Jacksonville, Fla.,"
full-figure alligator enm. bowl; "Jacksonville, Fla. Oliver
W. Jr.," ostrich enm. bowl; "Deland," alligator in swamp
enm. bowl.*

*Figure 5.11 Miami, spoons featuring Royal Palm Hotel,
palm tree trademark.*

*Figure 5.12 Enm. bowl spoons, variations on orange de-
signs, mkd. "Daytona," "Tampa," "Jacksonville," "St. Petersburg."*

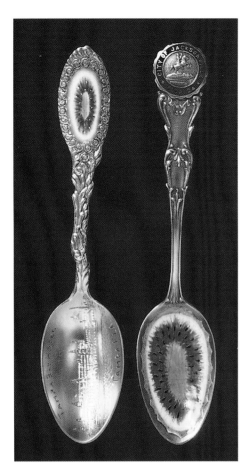

Figure 5.13 Enm. watermelon spoons: "Tampa Bay Hotel, Tampa, Fla." eng. bowl, enm. watermelon top; "City of Jacksonville Florida" enm. medallion and watermelon bowl.

Figure 5.14 Orange blossom enm. bowl with full-figure alligator, han. emb. "Florida."

Figure 5.15 "Jacksonville, Fla., Windsor Hotel" enm. bowl.; "St. Augustine, Fla., City Gates" enm. bowl.

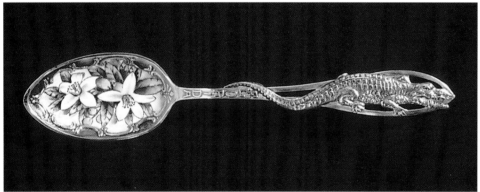

Florida's Golden Age of Souvenirs

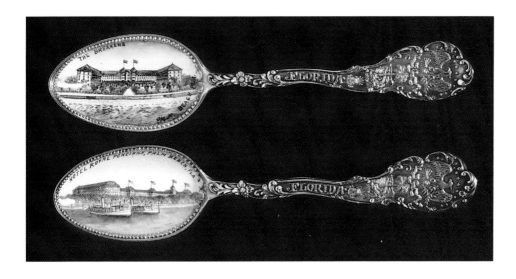

Figure 5.16 "Palm Beach, Fla., The Breakers" enm. bowl; "Palm Beach, Fla., Hotel Royal Poinciana" enm. bowl.

Figure 5.17 Set of four enm. alligator fruit forks, G&C cat., ca. 1900–1910.

Figure 5.18 "Palm Beach, Fla. Palm Avenue" emb. electroplated bowl; untitled, painted orange bowl, full-figure alligator han.

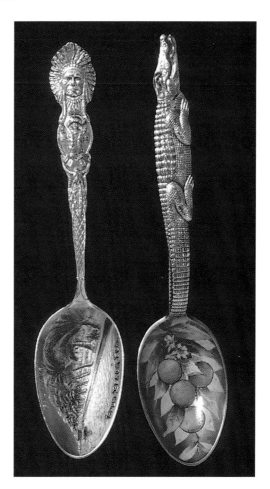

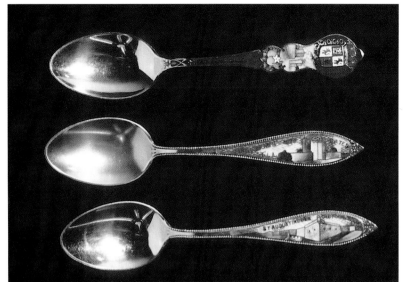

Figure 5.19 St. Augustine, full enm. han., Spanish crest, "Old City Gates, St. Augustine," "City Gates," "Old Fort Marion."

Figure 5.20 Poinsettia spoons: "Palm Beach, Fla." eng. bowl; "Miami, Fla." eng. bowl; "St. Petersburg, Fla." eng. bowl. with emb., enm. "Poinsettia."

Figure 5.21 Orange blossom enm. han.: "Sarasota Fla." eng. bowl; alligator, "Florida" emb. bowl; mossy oak, "Jacksonville, Fla." eng. bowl.

Figure 5.22 Orange enm. han.: "Jacksonville, Fla." eng. bowl; "Palm Beach, Fla." eng. bowl; plain bowl.

Figure 5.23 "St. Augustine, Florida, settled 1563" emb., enm. han.; "Ponce de Leon Hotel" emb. bowl; "Palm Beach" enm. bowl with enm. foliate decorated han., Spanish crest top.

Figure 5.24 Variations of enm. orange handle decorations: "St. Augustine, Fla." eng. bowl; "Jacksonville, Fla." eng. bowl; "Tampa, Fla." eng. bowl; "Winter Park, Fla. Seminole Chief" eng. bowl.; "St. Petersburg, Fla." eng. bowl; "The City Gates, St. Augustine, Fla." emb. bowl; "Tampa, Fla." eng. bowl.

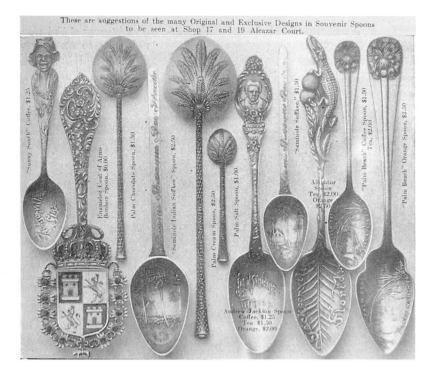

These are suggestions of the many Original and Exclusive Designs in Souvenir Spoons to be seen at Shop 17 and 19 Alcazar Court.

Figure 5.25 Spoons designed and sold by G&C, G&C cat., ca. 1900–1910.

Figure 5.26 Jacksonville, close-up of an acid-etched bowl, "Jacksonville, Fla."

Figure 5.27 Tampa, close-up of emb. bowl, "Tampa Bay Hotel."

Figure 5.28 Key West "rebus" spoon (rebus is representation of a word by an object whose name resembles it), key represents "Key" in "Key West."

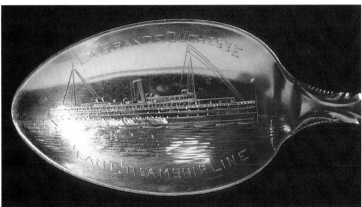

Figure 5.29 "The Magnolia" eng. bowl. Hotel was located on the St. Johns River, two miles north of Green Cove Springs.

Figure 5.30 "La Grande Duchesse, Plant Steamship Line" eng. bowl.

Figure 5.31 "St. Augustine" eng. bowl with enm. Spanish crest finial, 5 o'clock size; "Jacksonville, Fla." eng. bowl. with enm. Spanish crest top.

Figure 5.32 State seal enm. bowls, l to r, "Jacksonville," "Jacksonville" eng. on han., "Jacksonville."

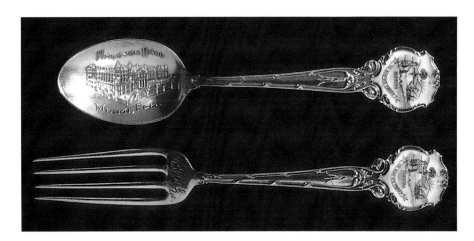

Figure 5.33 "Miami, Fla., Halcyon Hall" emb. bowl, Florida state seal medallion finial; "Key West" eng. just above fork tines, Florida state seal medallion at top.

Figure 5.34 Enm. han.: "La Grande Duchesse, Plant Steamship Line" eng. bowl, banana cluster top.; "Daytona" eng. bowl, enm. highlights on emb. bowl; "Rockledge, Indian River Fla." eng. bowl, entire spoon gold washed, with crossed Confederate and Cuban flags top; "Jacksonville, Fla." emb. bowl., enm. alligator top.

Figure 5.35 Enm. alligator han.: "Tampa Fla." eng. bowl; "Ormond" eng. bowl; "Hotel Punta Gorda, Fla." eng. bowl; "St. Augustine, Old City Gates" eng. bowl; "Tampa, Fla." eng. bowl; "Royal Palm Hotel, Miami, Fla." emb. bowl.

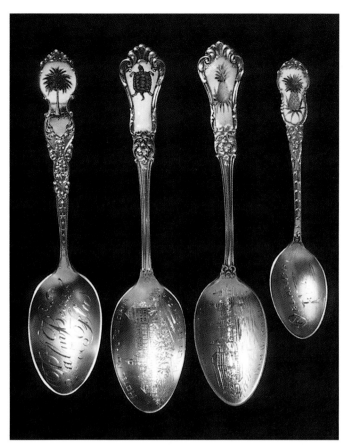

Figure 5.36 Enm. han.: "Palm Beach, Fla." eng. bowl., palm finial; "Hotel Royal Poinciana, Palm Beach, Fla." eng. bowl., turtle top; "Royal Poinciana Hotel, Palm Beach, Fla." eng. bowl, pineapple top; "Orlando, Fla." eng. bowl, pineapple finial, 5 o'clock spoon.

Figure 5.37 Die-cut enm. han.: "Florida" emb. han. with orange blossoms; "Miami, Florida" emb. han. with poinsettias; "Florida" emb. han. with banana tree.

Figure 5.38 Lemon fork, die cut, emb. "Florida" with enm. oranges.

Figure 5.39 Alligator han., die cut: "Florida" emb. han.; "Silver Springs" emb. han.; "Pensacola, Fla." emb. han., ca. 1915–1925.

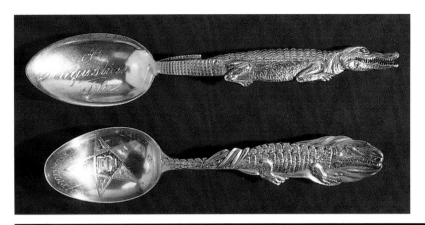

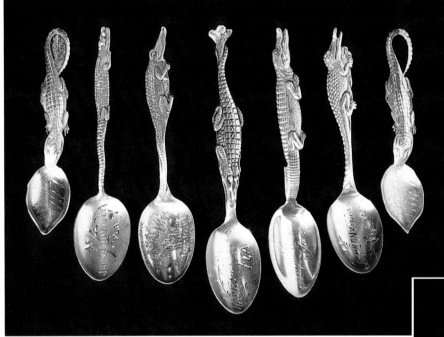

Figure 5.40 Full-figure alligator han.: "St. Augustine, Fla." eng. bowl; "Jacksonville, Fla. Eastern Star" eng. bowl.

Figure 5.41 Full-figure alligator han.: "St. Augustine Fla." acid-etched han., leaf pattern bowl; "Jacksonville, Fla." eng. bowl; "Banyan Tree, Key West, Fla." eng. bowl; "Jacksonville, Fla." eng. bowl; "St. Augustine, Fla." eng. bowl; "Jacksonville, Fla." eng. bowl; "Jacksonville, Fla." eng. bowl.

Figure 5.42 Alligator tooth han.: "Palm Beach, Fla." eng. bowl; "Miami, Fla." eng. bowl, both 5 o'clock size.

Figure 5.43 Black spoons: "Palm Beach, Fla." eng. bowl; "Jacksonville, Fla." eng. bowl; "Jacksonville, Fla." eng. bowl; "Key West, Fla." eng. bowl.

Figure 5.44 Black spoons: "St. Augustine" emb. bowl, "Sunny South" emb. han.; "Jacksonville, Fla." emb. bowl, "Sunny South" emb. han., gold-washed bowl and han. (spoons feature Johnny Griffin, a black boy who reportedly sold newspapers in front of the G&C store in Jacksonville, "adopted" as a "mascot" and the inspiration for "Sunny South" souvenirs designed and sold by G&C); "Gainesville, Fla. Court House" eng. bowl.

Figure 5.45 Black bowl close-up: "Rockledge, Uncle Tom" eng. bowl. oxidized to contrast image against silver.

Figure 5.46 Black spoons: "St. Augustine, Fla. Old City Gates" emb. bowl; "Jacksonville, Fla., Hemming Park" emb. bowl.

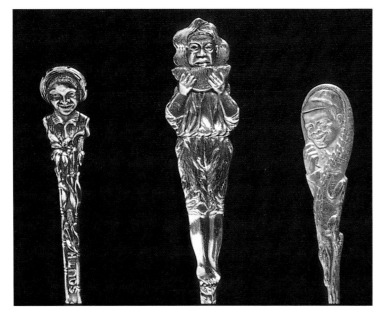

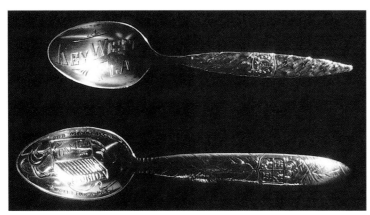

Figure 5.47 Black spoons: "Fernandina Fla." eng. bowl, "Sunny South" on han.; "Jacksonville, Fla." eng. bowl; "St. Augustine" emb. bowl.

Figure 5.48 Black spoons, enm. tops: "St. August-ine" eng. bowl; "Jacksonville Fla." eng. bowl, 5 o'clock size, both with gold-washed han. and bowls.

Figure 5.49 Cigar spoons, full-figure: "Key West, Fla." engraved in bowl, "Gato" engraved on cigar band on han. (Gato was one of Florida's leading ci-gar producers with factories in Key West and Tampa); "The Cigar City Tampa Florida A Million A Day" emb. bowl, Spanish crest emb. han.

Figure 5.50 Spanish American War: "Jacksonville, Fla. Camp Cuba Libre" eng. bowl, "Our Army" and bust of U.S. Army commander "General Miles" at top. Camp Cuba Libre was an army camp in Jacksonville set up to receive incoming troops for the war.

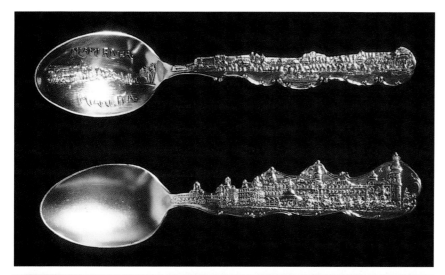

Figure 5.51 Skyline spoons: Miami skyline, "Miami River, Miami, Fla." emb. bowl; Tampa skyline plain bowl.

Figure 5.52 Historical figures: "Ponce de Leon," front and back; "St. Augustine" emb. bowl; "St. Augustine," "City Gates St. Augustine Fla." emb. bowl; figural finial "St. Augustine, A.D. 354430" emb. han, possibly a nun, "Jacksonville Fla. 1891" eng. bowl.

Figure 5.53 Ormond, Fla., "Ormond Hotel" eng. bowl, three-monkey han. (speak no evil, see no evil, hear no evil).

Figure 5.54 Political spoons: "Compliments of the Governor, Albert W. Gilcrest" eng. bowl, 3 monkeys soldered on back top of handle; "Compliments of Albert W. Gilcrest" eng. bowl, 3 monkeys soldered to bowl. Spoons reportedly given to graduates of Florida State College for Women when Gilcrest was governor, 1903–1913. The monkeys represent his motto, "Speak no evil, see no evil, hear no evil."

Figure 5.55 Constructed han.: "Tarpon Springs" eng. bowl; "Jacksonville, Fla." eng. bowl; "Sea Breeze, Fla." eng. bowl.

Figure 5.56 Constructed han.: "Tampa Bay Hotel, Tampa, Fla." eng. bowl; "Rockledge, Fla." eng. bowl, embossed alligator; "Rockledge Fla." engraved, gold-washed bowl.

Florida's Golden Age of Souvenirs

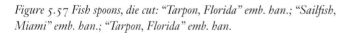

Figure 5.57 Fish spoons, die cut: "Tarpon, Florida" emb. han.; "Sailfish, Miami" emb. han.; "Tarpon, Florida" emb. han.

Figure 5.58 Fish spoons, die stamped: "Key West, Fla." eng. bowl; "Ft. Lauderdale, Fla." emb. bowl; "St. Petersburg, Fla." eng. bowl.

Figure 5.59 Indian finial spoons: "Jacksonville" emb. han., "1891" eng. on back; "Winter Park, Fla." eng. bowl; "Old City Gates St. Augustine," emb. bowl; "St. Augustine, Fla.," eng. han.; "Windsor Hotel, Jacksonville, Fla." emb. bowl, "Red Jacket" Indian finial, emb. han.

Figure 5.60 Full-figure Indians: "Palatka, Fla." eng. bowl; "City Gates, St. Augustine" emb. bowl; "Miami, Fla." eng. bowl.

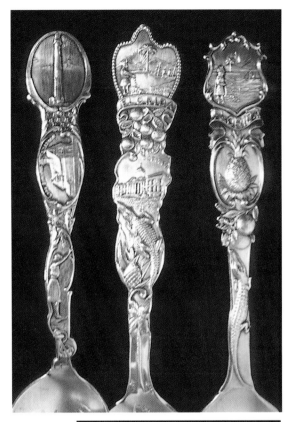

*Figure 5.61 Florida composite han.: "St. Petersburg Fla."
eng. bowl; "St. Petersburg" eng. bowl; "Jacksonville" eng.
bowl.*

*Figure 5.62 Florida spoons: "Pensacola, Fla." eng. bowl
gold washed with elaborate foliate han.; "Tampa Bay Hotel" han. and bowl acid etched (spoon purportedly made as
gift for hotel's grand opening); "Miami Biscayne Bay
Florida" emb. han.; "The Old Cape Florida Light" emb.
bowl, reverse, head of Osceola emb. on bowl; "Seminole
Soffkee Spoon" emb. han. "Soffkee" (the "Soffkee" spoon
was inspired by the ladle used to drink sofke, a warm corn
drink, a standard food of the Seminoles), G&C design.*

*Figure 5.63 Portrait finals: "Andrew Jackson Spoon,"
"Jacksonville, Florida" emb. bowl, "First Governor of
Florida 1821" emb. han., G&C design; "Osceola Chief,"
"Miami" emb. han.*

Figure 5.64 Five o'clock spoons: "Jacksonville, Fla." stippled bowl; "St. Augustine, Fla." eng. bowl, bird of paradise han.

Figure 5.65 Tampa: "Luna Via Tampa, Fla." emb. han., "Jules Verne" emb. bowl, patented 1891; same, eng. "Luna Via, Tampa" means "to the moon by way of Tampa." Spoon recognizes Jules Verne, author of From the Earth to the Moon, *published 1865, in which Tampa is site chosen for launch of manned space capsule to the moon.*

Figure 5.66 Handle variations: "Custom House & Post Office, Key West Fla." emb. bowl; "Kissimmee, Fla." eng. bowl, emb. lyrics han. "Den I Wish I Was in Dixie Hooray, Hooray"; "City Gates, St. Augustine, Fla." eng. bowl.

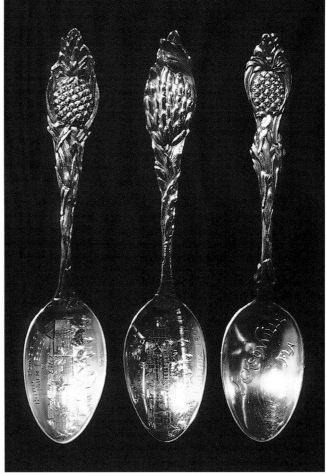

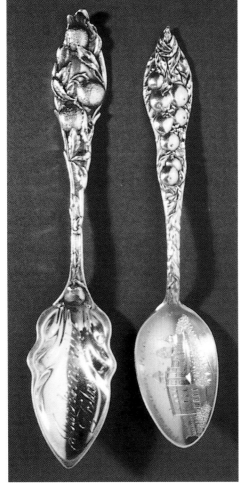

Figure 5.67 Serving spoons: "Hemming Park Jacksonville Fla." emb. bowl; "St. Augustine Fla." eng. bowl; "Old City Gates St. Augustine, Fla." emb. bowl.

Figure 5.68 Fruit finials: "Royal Poinciana Palm Beach Florida" eng. bowl; "Royal Poinciana Hotel, Palm Beach, Florida 1908" eng. bowl; "Jacksonville, Fla." emb. bowl.

Figure 5.69 Orange han.: "Jacksonville, Fla." eng. bowl; "Putnam House, Palatka, Fla." eng. bowl.

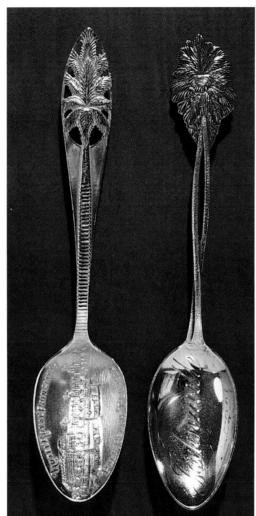

Figure 5.70 Palm Beach figural palm spoons: l, tea size; c., serving size, 8½"; r, 5 o'clock size. All emb. on back of han. "Palm Beach, Fla.," all G&C spoons.

Figure 5.71 Full palm handles: "Hotel Royal Poinciana, Palm Beach Florida," emb. bowl; "Jacksonville" eng. bowl.

Figure 5.72 Hand-cut large letter "Palm Beach, Fla."

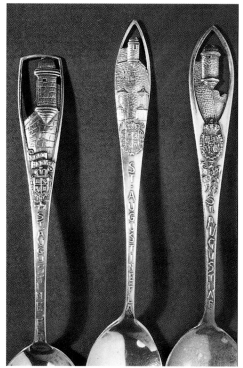

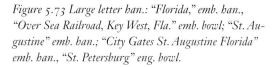

Figure 5.73 Large letter han.: "Florida," emb. han., "Over Sea Railroad, Key West, Fla." emb. bowl; "St. Augustine" emb. han.; "City Gates St. Augustine Florida" emb. han., "St. Petersburg" eng. bowl.

Figure 5.74 St. Augustine die-cut han.: "Fort Marion St. Augustine, Fla." emb. han.; "Fort Marion, St. Augustine" emb. han.; "Fort Marion, 1565, St. Augustine, Fla." emb. han.

Figure 5.75 St. Augustine types: "St. Augustine, Fla." eng. han.; "St. Augustine Fla." emb. han.; "St. Augustine, Fla." eng. han., "Ponce de Leon Hotel" eng. bowl; "St. Augustine" emb. han., "St. Augustine, Fla., Old Fort Marion, Old City Gates" eng. bowl; "Old Watch Tower, Fort Marion" emb. han.

Figure 5.76 Die-cut emb. han.: "Bellview Hotel, Florida"; "Tampa Bay Hotel, Tampa, Fla."; "Lafayette Street Bridge, Tampa, Fla."

Figure 5.77 Jacksonville spoons: "Waterfront, Jacksonville, Fla." emb. han.; "Hemming Park, Jacksonville, Fla." emb. han.; variation of preceding spoon.

Figure 5.78 Miami spoons, emb. han.: "Miami, Fla.," Seminoles in canoe; "The Flamingo Miami Beach, Fla."; "Hotel Royal Palm Miami Fla."

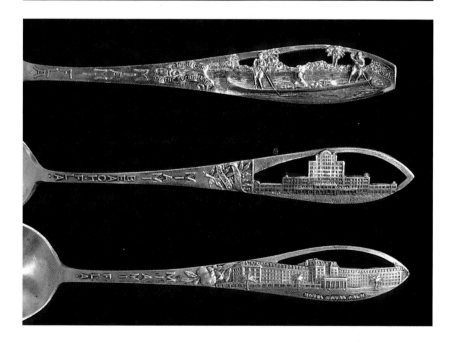

Figure 5.79 Fruit knives: full alligator han.; orange blossoms, G&C; oranges, leaves, and blossoms, G&C.

Figure 5.80 Full-figure alligator fruit knife, G&C cat., ca. 1900–1910. Forked knife tip specially designed to remove seeds.

Figure 5.81 Fruit knives: han. cameo view of "Watch Tower Ft. Marion," enm. Spanish crest, "El Unico, St. Augustine, Palm Beach Fla." stamped on blade; han. oranges, leaves, and blossoms and Old City Gates, G&C cat., ca. 1900–1910.

Figure 5.82 Fruit knives: celluloid han., oranges, leaves, and blossoms and Old City Gates; City Gates cameo, El Unico cat., 1898 (first and third knives celluloid copies of G&C silver han.).

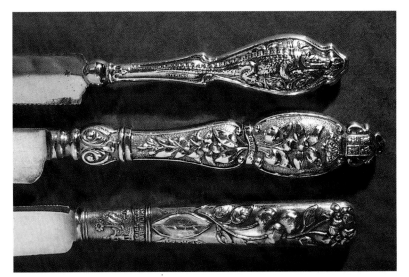

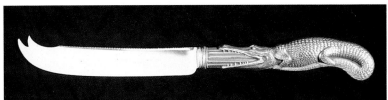

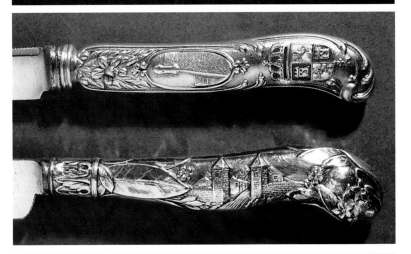

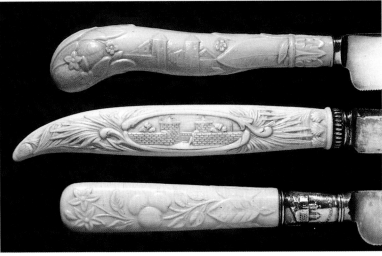

Florida's Golden Age of Souvenirs

Carved Alligator Souvenirs

Alligators have always been Florida's greatest natural attraction. Mysterious and maligned, they captured the readers' interest fueled by writers with vivid imaginations. From John Bartram's fanciful eighteenth-century tales to the sensational Victorian periodicals, alligators made good press. They also made good curios. They were stuffed or made into lamps, card holders, or ashtrays. Their teeth were used for jewelry, their hides and feet for purses.

Though I could find no reference to alligator curios prior to the Civil War, it is almost certain that stickpins, fobs, and other simple ornaments were made from alligator teeth. Similar mementos were popular after the revival of tourism in the 1870s. By the 1880s carved alligator souvenirs were becoming widely admired and were available at most tourist shops.

In 1895 Ralph Julian mentions in his book *Dixie, Southern Scenes and Sketches* that Bay Street in Jacksonville could be called "Alligator Avenue" because of all the saurian souvenirs sold there. He wrote, "Figures of them were carved on canes, molded on souvenir spoons, painted on china, and sold in the form of photographs and watercolor studies, breast pins and carvings."

Most likely, the first carved alligator appeared on a cane, as walking sticks were exceedingly popular throughout the nineteenth century. As early as 1838 a tourist visiting the Florida House in St. Augustine notes, "Along the sunny side of the hotel I saw invalids cutting and whittling orange sticks for canes to take back home as presents." No doubt alligators would be a fine subject for the orangewood shafts, with their long slender shapes well suited to the form.

Advertisements from regional publications and city directories from the 1870s indicate that Jacksonville was becoming the production center for alligator canes and other saurian souvenirs. Florida's booming tourist trade offered an ideal economic base for such carved goods.

By the 1880s commercially made alligator canes had become quite fashionable, appealing to women as well as to men. Most were made from readily available orangewood "suckers." These were the unwanted shoots that grew on citrus trees and were cut off and discarded by the growers. They were usually straight, ideal for cane shafts and handles. In 1884 James Henshall makes an interesting reference to canes in his book *Camping and Cruising in Florida*. While outfitting for his trip in Jacksonville, he states, "I proceeded to look up my companions and found Ben in a canemaker's shop intently watching the man carving alligators on the tops of orangewood canes." Orangewood was used in making Florida "sticks" and can be identified by the irregular knobs running the length of the cane's shaft.

Other Florida woods such as hickory, various palms, sapodilla, snakewood, and princewood were also used for shafts. The more expensive canes had handles made of stag or buck horn as well as bone and ivory. These were sometimes stained brown or green to give the carved gators a more realistic appearance. A surviving Osky's souvenir catalogue dating ca. 1910–1915 offers orangewood alligator handle canes for seventy-five cents each and ivory ones for six dollars.

Many of the canes attributed to Jacksonville commercial carvers are identifiable from recurring stylistic elements that can be recognized in the treatment of the alligator's head, eyes, feet, body position, and overall creative presence. These stylistic similarities are reflected in other carved gator souvenirs as well, especially pipes and corkscrews.

As early as 1875 the Greenleaf and Crosby Company of Jacksonville was advertising walking sticks. One ad touts "walking canes of all kinds of Florida wood, carved and plain." A search of old Jacksonville city directories revealed several "walking stick" and "cane" manufacturers plus one "carver." The earliest reference appears in an 1876–1877 issue and notes a Dick Williams as a "walking stick" manufacturer. By 1882 another directory lists Beach and Rancon as well as the Skilton Brothers as cane makers, and Clark Wilson as a carver. A directory from 1886 notes cane makers Levy and Samuel Joiner, who would be joined by Samuel Joiner Jr. the following year. John B. Ross was listed as a carver in 1887.

An introduction from an 1882 Jacksonville directory states that the manufacture of "canes" and of "carved goods," that is, alligator souvenirs, was among the city's primary industries. These items became so popular that by the 1890s Jacksonville manufacturers were selling them nationwide.

Probably the largest company to focus on alligator goods was Osky's of Jacksonville. Founded in 1884, the firm operated from its storefront on Bay Street until 1955. Fortunately, three different Osky's catalogues remain from the Golden Age. They reveal an amazing array of novelties, with at least eighty items sporting carved alligators, including canes, clocks, manicure sets, whistles, inkwells, corkscrews, and jewelry. The majority of these were made from orangewood, but materials such as shell, bone, horn, ivory, and pearwood were used as well. Much of the jewelry was fashioned from alligator teeth. Sometimes town and state names were added in India ink to identify their place of purchase.

The end of World War I marked the decline of cane production and alligator carving in Jacksonville. A search of the city directories shows no cane manufacturers after the war.

Carved alligator souvenirs were among Florida's most prominent mementos. They were sold statewide, and many survive today—proof of their former popularity. Today the gator canes and other similar souvenirs offer a rare opportunity to collect some of Florida's best nineteenth- and early twentieth-century folk art. Though most were commercially produced, each maintains its individuality, defined by the hand of the carver.

Figure 6.1 Postcard of "Bay Street" in Jacksonville when known as "Alligator Avenue" or "Curio Row," ca. 1900–1910.

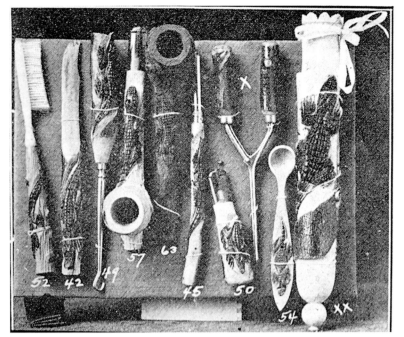

Figure 6.2 Osky's cat. illustration, ca. 1905–1915, cvd. alligator souvenirs made from orangewood.

Figure 6.3 Osky's cat. illustration, ca. 1905–1915, cvd. alligator souvenirs made from ivory and bone.

Figure 6.4 Cane han.: bone, 5¾", orangewood shaft; ivory, 3¾", black palm shaft.

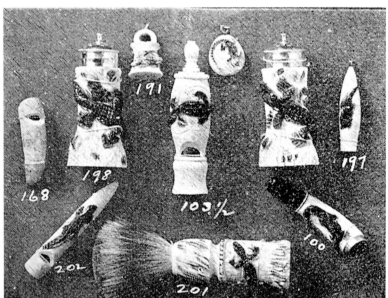

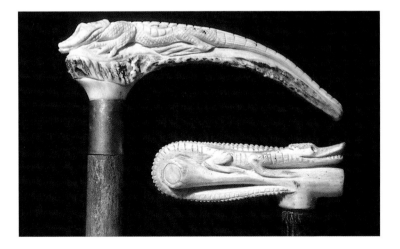

Florida's Golden Age of Souvenirs

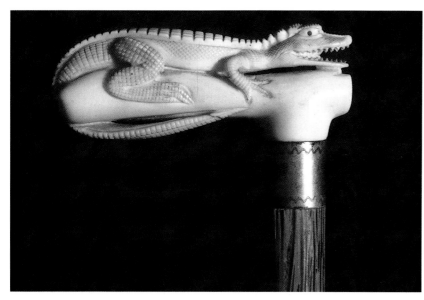

Figure 6.5 Cane han., ivory, 3¾", palm wood shaft, $6.00 in Osky's cat., ca. 1900–1910.

Figure 6.6 Cane han.: ivory sphinxlike alligator, 4", wood unidentified; ivory, 4¼", fancy silver collar, mahogany shaft.

Figure 6.7 Cane han., ivory, 5", faux bamboo shaft, $6.00 in Osky's cat., ca. 1900–1910. Light, elegant cane probably designed for women. Victorian-era fashion had woman as well as children carrying canes.

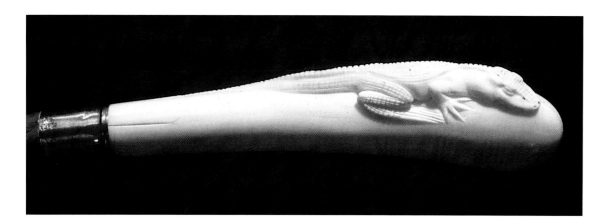

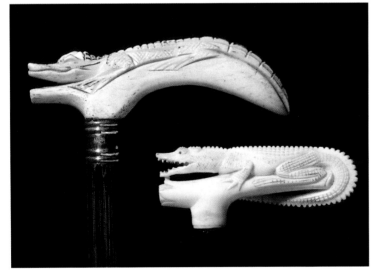

Top left: *Figure 6.8 Cane han.: t, deer antler, 5″; b, ivory, 4 ¼″, hickory shaft.*

Bottom left: *Figure 6.9 Cane han.: bone, 3 ½″, shaft wood unidentified; ivory, 2 ¾″, ebony shaft. Small size suggests either swagger sticks or children's canes.*

Top right: *Figure 6.10 Variations of orange-wood alligator han. and shafts.*

Florida's Golden Age of Souvenirs

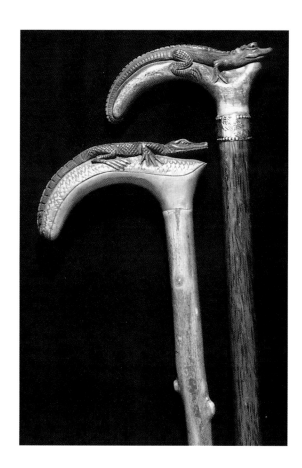

Figure 6.11 Cane han.: orangewood, 4¾", orangewood shaft; orangewood, 4¾", "St. Augustine, Fla." emb. around silver collar, palm wood shaft, sold by G&C.

Figure 6.12 Cane han.: t, alligator head emerging from han.; b, unusual hook shape used to pull fruit from orange trees, both with orangewood han. and shafts.

Figure 6.13 Varieties of alligator cane han.: c, orangewood.

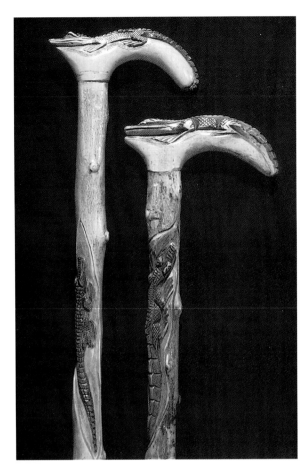
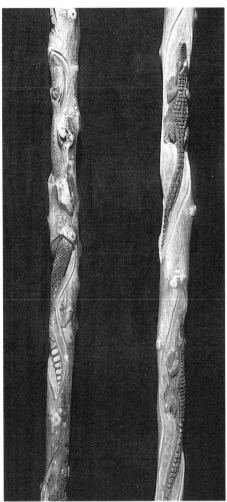

Figure 6.14 Orangewood canes with alligator han. and multiple gator shafts: t, alligator near shaft top, alligator near bottom with rattlesnake; b, three equal sized gators cvd. down shaft. $1.25 in Osky's cat., ca. 1905–1915.

Figure 6.14a Details of shafts, Figure 6.14.

Figure 6.15 Polychrome alligator canes: t, black background contrasts with natural orangewood color of cvd. alligators; b, four alligators painted black against natural wood background, positioned equally down the shaft.

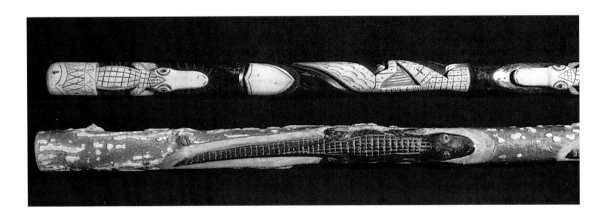

Florida's Golden Age of Souvenirs

Figure 6.16 Close-ups of richly detailed polychrome orangewood cane featuring alligators, frogs, rattlesnake.

Figure 6.17 Swagger stick, cvd. Turkshead han. with silver plaque "Florida Orangewood, Presented to Ira Re?ol by S. C. Bullard."

Figure 6.17a Detail of plaque, Figure 6.17.

Figure 6.18 Black boy and alligator polychrome pipe, orangewood, 11", boy's head, hands, and feet ebony. This and next three pipes illustrate common themes used by Jacksonville carvers.

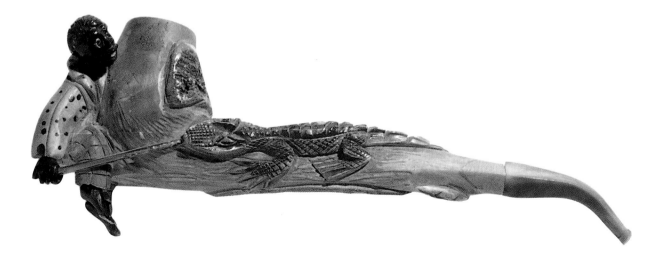

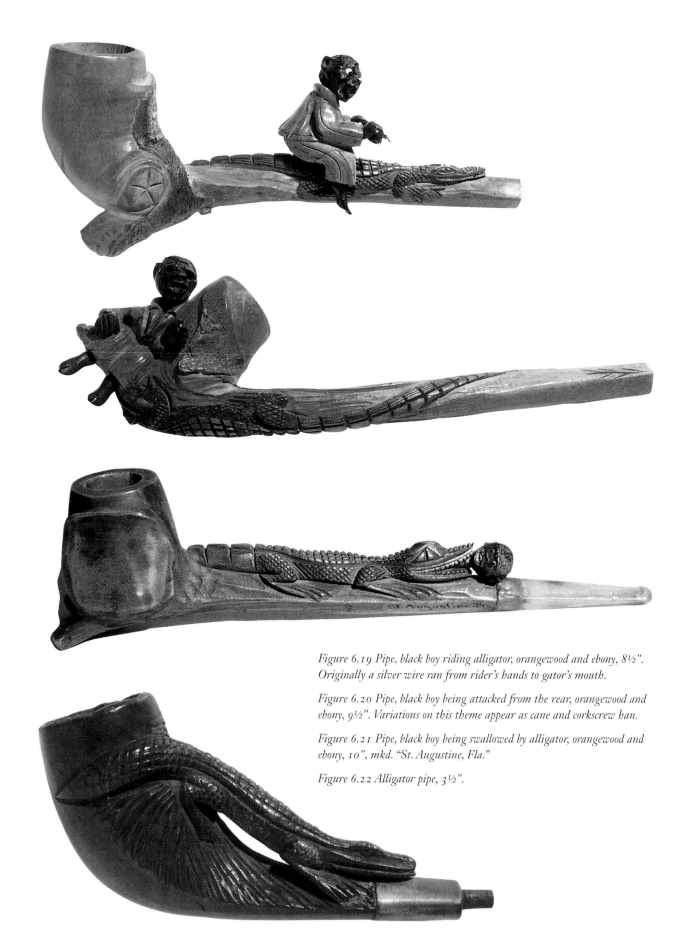

Figure 6.19 Pipe, black boy riding alligator, orangewood and ebony, 8½″. Originally a silver wire ran from rider's hands to gator's mouth.

Figure 6.20 Pipe, black boy being attacked from the rear, orangewood and ebony, 9½″. Variations on this theme appear as cane and corkscrew han.

Figure 6.21 Pipe, black boy being swallowed by alligator, orangewood and ebony, 10″, mkd. "St. Augustine, Fla."

Figure 6.22 Alligator pipe, 3½″.

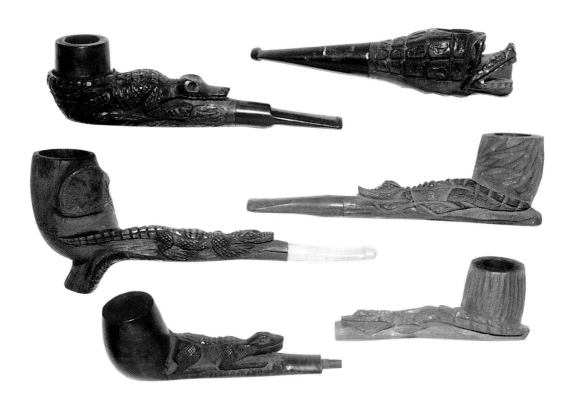

Figure 6.23 Alligator pipes, 4" to 8"; Osky's cat., ca. 1913, lists 4" gator pipes at fifty cents each.

Figure 6.24 Alligator corkscrew, deer antler, 6½", $1.25 in Osky's cat., ca. 1913.

Figure 6.25 Alligator corkscrew, boar's tusk with silver cap, 10".

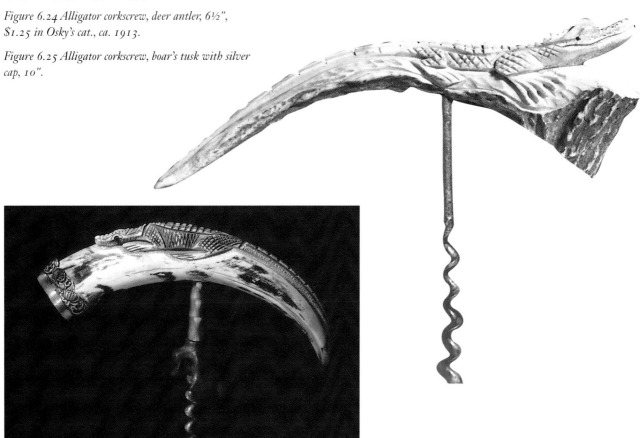

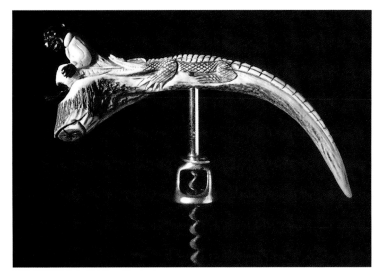

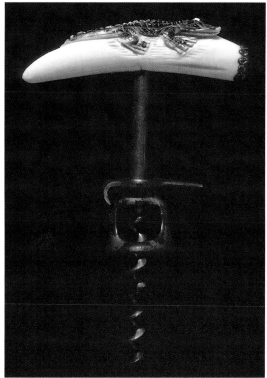

Figure 6.26 Black boy and alligator corkscrew, deer antler, 11", boy's head, hands, and feet ebony, inset glass eyes.

Figure 6.27 Alligator corkscrew, 4¼", cvd. on small sperm whale's tooth, silver cap on end, $2.50–$4.00, depending on size, in Osky's cat., ca. 1900–1910.

Figure 6.28 Salad sets: large, 11"; small, 4", Osky's cat., ca. 1913.

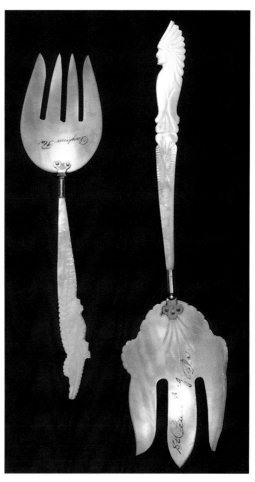

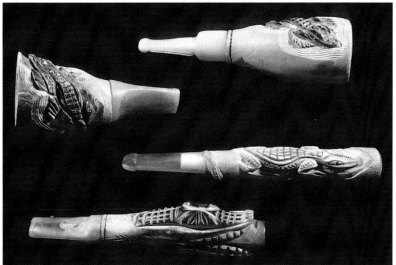

Figure 6.29 Spoons, l, *mother of pearl, 9",
han. signed in India ink "Tampa, Fla."; r,
orangewood han., mother of pearl bowl,
9½".*

Figure 6.30 Serving forks, *mother of
pearl: t, cvd. alligator han. mkd. "Daytona,
Fla.," 7½"; b, cvd. Indian han. mkd. "St.
Petersburg, Fla.," 9½".*

Figure 6.31 *Cigar and cigarette holders,
3"–4½".*

Figure 6.32 Alligator whimsy, 5 ¾", inset glass eyes, white-painted teeth.

Figure 6.33 Orangewood doorpull, 14".

Figure 6.34 Pair of bone vases, 7 ¼".

Florida's Golden Age of Souvenirs

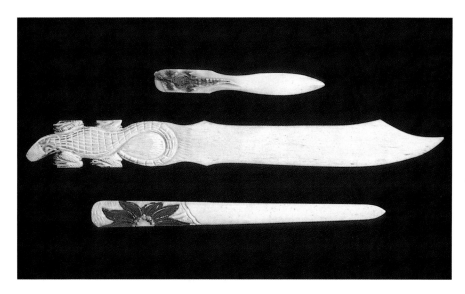

Figure 6.35 Letter openers: ivory, 4"; bone, 10"; bone, 7", Osky's cat., ca. 1905–1915.

Figure 6.36 Letter openers: bone with brass alligator han., 4¼"; mother of pearl, 5"; mother of pearl mkd. "St. Augustine," 6¾".

Figure 6.37 Cvd. alligator ink pens: t, mother of pearl mkd. "Key West, Fla."; b, bone.

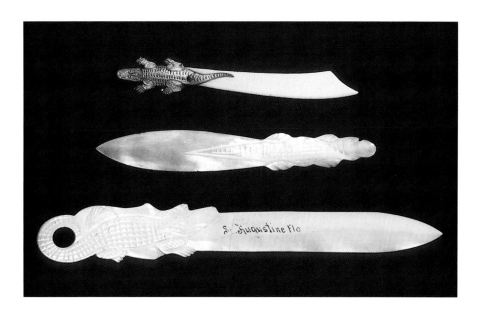

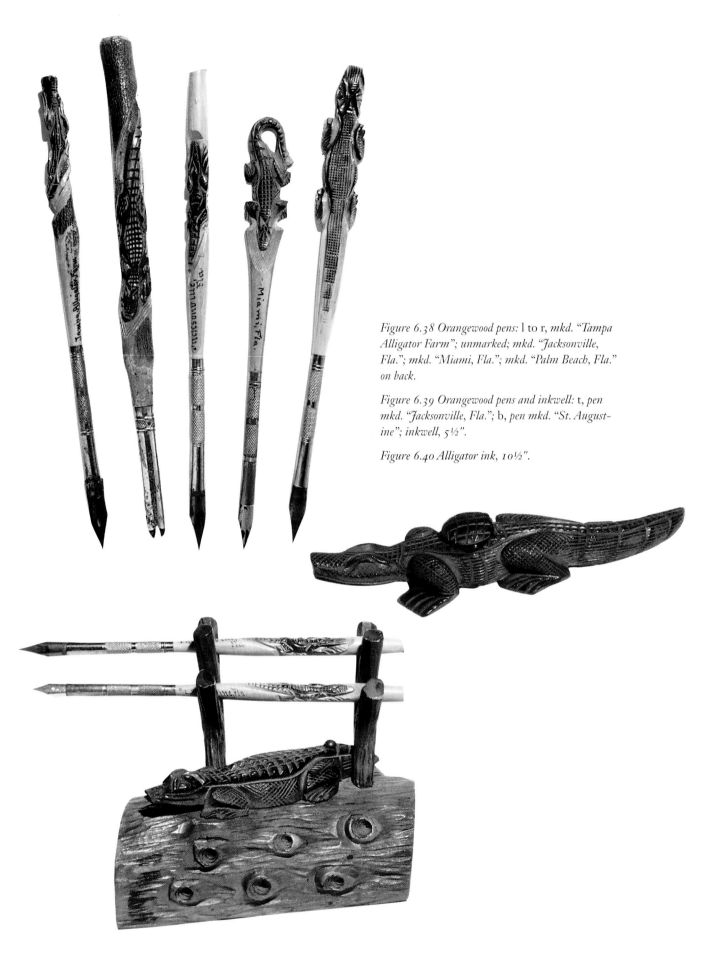

Figure 6.38 Orangewood pens: l to r, mkd. "Tampa Alligator Farm"; unmarked; mkd. "Jacksonville, Fla."; mkd. "Miami, Fla."; mkd. "Palm Beach, Fla." on back.

Figure 6.39 Orangewood pens and inkwell: t, pen mkd. "Jacksonville, Fla."; b, pen mkd. "St. Augustine"; inkwell, 5½".

Figure 6.40 Alligator ink, 10½".

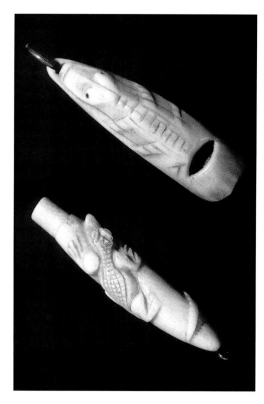

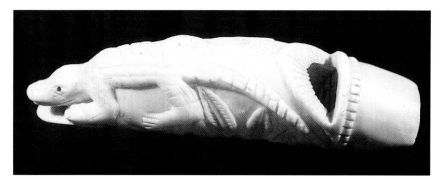

Figure 6.41 Standing gator penrest and pen with black boy head finial, 4½", ca. 1900–1910.

Figure 6.42 Cvd. alligator tooth whistle, ca. 1890–1900, 2¾".

Figure 6.43 Cvd. alligator whistle and pin, both 1½".

Figure 6.44 Alligator tooth whistle and perfume, both 2".

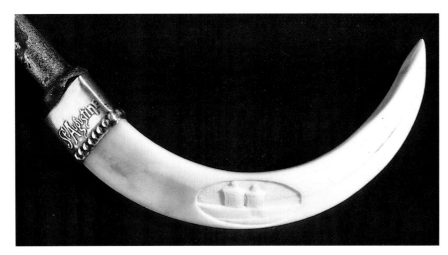

Figure 6.45 Gator whistles, l to r, gator tooth; bone mkd. "St. Petersburg, Fla."; orangewood; stained orangewood; orangewood mkd. "Silver Springs, Fla."; nos. 2, 3, and 4, Osky's cat., ca. 1905–1915; no. 5, ca. 1920–30. Size range 2¾"–3½".

Figure 6.46 Boar's tusk buttonhook, cvd. cameo of City Gates, "St. Augustine" around sterling mount, ca. 1890–1900.

Figure 6.47 Boar's tusk han., similar to han. on button hook, Figure 6.46.

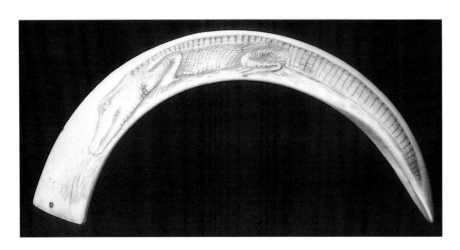

Figure 6.48 Orangewood hatpin holder, 8″, $1.00 in Osky's cat., ca. 1913.

Figure 6.49 Tobacco humidor, cvd. alligator body added to halved and hinged coconut, 11¾″.

Figure 6.50 Orangewood stein, 10½″, ca. 1900–1910, excellent example of Jacksonville carving.

Figure 6.51 Three Alligator souvenirs: orangewood napkin ring, 2″; bone salt shaker, 2 ⅝″; orangewood toothpick holder, 2″.

Figure 6.52 Orangewood napkin rings, 1 ¼″–1 ½″, ca. 1905–1915.

Figure 6.53 Snake pipe rack, 18″, Osky's cat., ca. 1905–1915.

Florida's Golden Age of Souvenirs

Harris and Barnhill Prints

By the turn of the century Florida had become a winter haven for many itinerant artists, including photographers. Florida's green graces offered many photographic opportunities lost in the bleak, snowy winters of the north. The state was a beckoning paradise waiting to be captured through the photographer's lens.

Around 1900 Wallace Nutting, a Connecticut preacher, began making a name for himself as a photographer. He specialized in hand-tinted New England landscapes, though a few Florida examples are known. By the 1920s his work had become exceedingly popular, with millions of his pictures selling throughout the United States. Nutting's work had a profound influence on a number of Florida landscape photographers.

Among them two stand out, not only for their Florida scenes but for their existing bodies of work. One was W. J. Harris, who was located in St. Augustine. The other was E. G. Barnhill, in St. Petersburg. Both used water colors as their chosen medium. Of the two, Harris appears to have produced the greater number of prints. In my eighteen years as a Harris-Barnhill collector, I've seen perhaps 125 different Harris pictures and approximately 40–50 Barnhills. There's also a good indication that a greater variety of Harris prints exist because of numbered ordering tags that have remained attached to the backs of some of the pictures. I have seen numbers as low as 14, as high as 701, and in between, suggesting a series with at least 701 different views. However, this number could include numbers assigned for variations in individual picture size, which would reduce the actual count.

Although Harris and Barnhill both made hand-colored pictures and used similar subject matter, their works are fairly easy to distinguish from one another. Harris pictures incorporated soft pastel tints, airbrushed to create gently muted colors. Barnhill, on the other hand, used richer tones, resulting in a darker format. To better understand the two artists, a look at their backgrounds will help.

William James Harris, 1868–1940

W. J. Harris was born in Herefordshire, England, in 1868. In 1870 his family emigrated to America and settled in or near Wilkes-Barre, Pennsylvania. By the time he graduated from high school he had become interested in art and was drawn to photography in particular. By 1886 or early the following year, young Will would open his first studio.

At the time it was customary for photographers to travel, offering their services as they went. Harris readily embraced the prospects of such a life. He wandered across the Northeast, working for the most part in Pennsylvania, New York, and New Jersey, catering to the tourist trade and setting up his portable studio as the seasons dictated. He went to Chicago in 1893 and photographed parts of the Columbian Exposition, which as we have seen, was the catalyst of the souvenir trade.

This course would eventually lead him to Florida. In 1898 W. J. would make his first trip to St. Augustine, at the age of twenty-nine. This he did as operator and manager of the Acme View Company of Pittstown, Pennsylvania. The studio was located on St. George Street, where Harris developed film for amateurs and sold photographic supplies, including cameras. To encourage business he gave beginners free instructions and use of the shop darkroom.

Harris soon began photographing St. Augustine landmarks and the exotic wildlife that drew tourists to the area. Most of these photos would be made into postcards, his primary source of income before he began to distribute his prints.

That same year, 1898, as the winter season was closing and with summer on its way, Harris left St. Augustine for New Jersey. He had heard of the lucrative prospects of Lake Hopatcong, an established playground for the wealthy. He soon opened a lakeside studio that proved very successful.

This winter/summer shift between Florida and New Jersey would ultimately become the pulse of Harris's life. From about 1900 to 1913 he sold mostly postcards and his services as a photographer. However, by 1911, he began shifting his talent toward hand-colored souvenir photographs. At this time, his photos focused on old St. Augustine and its picturesque surroundings, with views of Ft. Marion being the most popular.

Harris began tinting photos in 1905, during one of his summer visits to Lake Hopatcong. It may have been around this time that he began coloring his Florida pictures. By 1911 he was reproducing some of his postcards using a copying process known as gravure printing. This coincides with his focus on hand tinted "Harris pictures" and was probably when he began using photogravure printing to replicate his images.

By 1926 Harris had several skilled artists busily tinting his pictures. Many of the prints were rectangular, approximately twice as long as they were wide. They range in size from 2" x 5" to 6 1/2" x 16 1/2." Others came in a standard 7 1/2" x 9 1/2" size, more square shaped than rectangular. However, these are not precise dimensions but rather guidelines, as it is common for these pictures to vary by at least one-eighth of an inch.

The majority of the prints were mounted on thin cardboard stock with an impressed recess slightly larger than the print. This created an embossed margin around the image that helped accentuate the picture. Usually the penciled signatures and titles were placed just under the print at opposite corners and within the indented margin. An experienced collector will notice that there are often variations in handwriting on individual prints. Harris at one time employed as many as seven airbrush artists to color his pictures. When they finished tinting the images, they titled them and signed Harris's name, thus producing the differences in signatures. Sometimes Harris took the negative of a particularly popular scene, reversed it, and gave it a new title, thus creating a "mirror image" picture. At other times his pictures would fill the complete frame and his name and title would appear in white ink at the bottom corners of the print.

Harris traveled much of Florida's east coast in search of new images for his popular pictures. He had a specially converted REO speedwagon that served as a house-car and portable studio. He also had a small cabin boat called the *Porpoise* from which he photographed the Tomoka, Indian, and Ocklawaha Rivers.

We know from his work that he must have ventured into the central part of the state and even the Gulf coast, as pictures, though rare, exist of Lake Lucerne in Orlando, Lake Dora in Mt. Dora, DeLeon Springs, St. Petersburg, and more commonly Bok Tower, in Lake Wales. Outside of his charming views of St. Augustine's historic buildings and landmarks, Harris limited most of his pictures to Florida landscapes.

Though Harris only wintered in St. Augustine, he had a significant influence on this quaint city. He became involved with the historical society, both as a promoter of St. Augustine tourism and as an influential businessman. His lasting relationship with the society proved lucrative and beneficial. Through the auspices of the historical society, Harris gained an exclusive lease for old Ft. Marion in 1914. Here he set up shop selling local souvenirs and his Harris pictures.

From Harris's introduction of tinted photographs around 1911 until his death, August 7, 1940, Harris pictures would remain the mainstay of his business. His pastel palette tamed Florida's formidable wilds and portrayed a fresh and embracing Eden that welcomed all to the sunny South.

Esmond G. Barnhill, 1894–1987

Esmond G. Barnhill was born in the small North Carolina town of Saluda on March 4, 1894. As a child he became an avid collector of American Indian artifacts, which led to a lifelong passion for archeology and treasure hunting.

By his late teens Barnhill had developed a keen interest in photography, and he would soon join the ranks of traveling photographers. By 1914 he had made his way to Florida, settling in St. Petersburg. His first shop was called the Florida Photo Studio and was located at Third Street North and Tenth Avenue. Like Harris, he began by selling postcards and colored pictures.

Before coming to Florida Barnhill tried his hand as an "Indian trader" in Estes Park, Colorado, where he opened a curio shop specializing in American Indian artifacts and Native American crafts. While there he met and worked with renowned photographer Edward Curtis. It was Curtis who introduced him to tinting images, specifically to a process called "goldtoning." This was done by coloring the photographic images on the glass negative with special uranium dyes. When this stage was completed, the back of the glass was covered in a gold-foil-like sealant, which gave it a golden glow that seemed to illuminate the picture. Most of Barnhill's goldtone images are titled on the back and bear the date 1914. This date may not reflect the actual year he finished the picture, as Barnhill postdated much of his work. Still, these images are among his earliest Florida works and date from around 1914 to the early 1920s.

About this time Barnhill began hand tinting printed copies of his photographs. He had used the Albertype Company in New York to publish his postcards and probably used them to replicate his uncolored prints. While Harris tinted his pictures using an airbrush, Barnhill chose to use hand-applied water colors. This method resulted in the rich undiluted colors common to his prints. They came in a variety of sizes ranging from 2" x 5 1/2" to 9" x 10," and some were matted in the same fashion as Harris prints, with Barnhill's signature and picture title in opposing corners at the bottom of the image.

Like Harris, he preferred Florida landscapes over other subjects, but he did offer a line of greeting cards featuring Ft. Marion in St. Augustine. Most of Barnhill's hand-colored prints and greeting cards date from c. 1920 to c. 1930.

In 1915 Barnhill purchased the remaining prints of James Ralph Wilcox, a Florida landscape photographer and picture colorist who had died that year at the age of forty-nine. Wilcox's studio was in Seabreeze (now Daytona) and well stocked with Florida landscape prints, both tinted and untinted. Though Wilcox's landscapes were similar to Barnhill's, his concept of coloration was noticeably different. Barnhill chose bold contrasting colors, while Wilcox's work reflected softer, more muted tones. Many of Wilcox's untinted prints were hand colored by Barnhill. He even signed Wilcox's name and added the date 1890. This is particularly curious as Wilcox first visited Florida in 1901 but didn't move to the state until 1905. Still, it is fairly simple to tell the signatures apart. Wilcox signed his name with a distinct tilt to the left, while the Barnhill forgeries are perpendicular.

By 1935 Barnhill was no longer listed as a photographer in the St. Petersburg city directory, but he was still registered as owning the Barnhill Camera Shop and selling photographic equipment supplies. By the mid-1930s Barnhill's business began to shift from photography to photographic supplies, but the change was relatively short-lived, as there was no mention of Barnhill in the directories after 1936. Instead, his wife, Helen, appeared as owner of a gift shop. By 1938 Helen still owned her shop but was listed as living in Dania, Florida, probably relegating day-to-day business to one of her two sons.

This information places the Barnhills in Dania in 1938. Around World War II Barnhill decided to open another Indian Trading Post similar to his first one in Colorado, this time in Wisconsin Dells, Wisconsin. He ran this during the summers until 1959. This was followed by another trading post in Booth Bay Harbor, Maine, and another in Indian Springs, Georgia. In 1953 Barnhill opened an attraction called Ancient America in Boca Raton, Florida. This closed in 1958. From here he moved to Palm Bay, Florida, near Cocoa, where he established a museum to exhibit his collections of artifacts and "pirate treasures."

His final roadside venture was the Indian Museum and Trading Post opened in 1970 near Kissimmee, Florida. He chose this location because of its proximity to the soon to be opened Disney World. The business closed in the mid 1980s, and Barnhill moved to North Georgia. He died in 1987 at the age of ninety-three.

It appears that most of Barnhill's pictures were produced from ca. 1914 to ca. 1930. Though he didn't have the variety of pictures Harris did, he produced a much greater volume. For some reason much of his stock never sold, and when his estate was liquidated a large number of his prints were discovered and purchased by local antique dealers. Because of this circumstance, the bulk of his work remains in Florida and can still be found in a few shops from the central part of the state to Palm Beach.

Barnhill was a consummate blend of artist, adventurer, and entrepreneur. He traveled Florida, the Caribbean islands, and Panama in search of artifacts and treasures. What began as a photographic enterprise evolved into a series of Indian trading post–museum roadside attractions. These in turn drew the curious tourists to buy his prints, postcards, and other souvenirs that collectors seek today.

*Figure 7.1 "Leaning Moss Oak,
Fla." 7″ x 9″. Harris reversed
this scene and called it "Leaning
Oaks."*

*Figure 7.2 "Palm River, Fla.," by Harris,
7⅛″ x 9½″.*

Figure 7.3 "Lake Howard, Winter Haven, Fla.," by Harris, 6½" x 16¼".

Figure 7.4 "Mirror Lake, St. Petersburg, Fla.," by Harris, 6½" x 16½".

Figure 7.5 "Royal Palm Grove, Fla.," by Harris, 6⅜" x 16⅜".

Figure 7.6 "To the Garden of Eden, Fla.," by Harris,
6½" x 16½", picture no. 548.

Figure 7.7 "Florida Sunset," by Harris, 6½" x 16½".

Figure 7.8 "On The Suwannee River," by Harris,
7¼" x 9¼". A hand-colored photograph rather than
the more common hand tinted gravure prints, ca.
1910–1920.

Figure 7.9 "Beach Scene, St. Augustine, Fla.," by Harris, 3" x 6⅞".

Figure 7.10 "Florida Sunset," by Harris, 7½" x 9½". Note same title as Figure 7.7.

Figure 7.11 "Orange Grove, Fla.," by Harris, 6½" x 16¼".

Figure 7.12 "Tomoka Point, Fla.," by Harris, 7½" x 9".

Figure 7.13 "Cape Florida," by Harris, 7½" x 9". Cape Florida lighthouse is on Biscayne Bay, Miami.

Figure 7.14 "Live Oak and Palmetto, Florida," by Harris, 6¼" x 16¼".

Figure 7.15 "Fort Marion, St. Augustine, Fla.," by Harris, 3" x 5". Left corner imprinted "C 1912 Harris."

Figure 7.16 "Fountain of Youth, St. Augustine, Florida," by Harris, 7½" x 9".

Figure 7.17 "Tomoka River, Fla.," by Harris, 1924 calendar; print size 3″ x 7″.

Figure 7.18 "DeLeon Springs, Fla.," by Harris, 3″ x 7″.

Figure 7.19 "Palmetto Point, Florida," by Harris, 7½″ x 9″.

Florida's Golden Age of Souvenirs

Figure 7.20 "River Palm, Fla.," by Harris, 6½" x 16¼".

Figure 7.21 "Under the Florida Moss," by Harris, 6½" x 12½".

Figure 7.22 "Florida Palms," by Harris, 7¼" x 9¼".

Figure 7.23 "Garden—Oldest School House, St. Augustine Florida," by Harris, 7½" x 9½".

Figure 7.24 Example of Harris label commonly attached to backs of prints.

Figure 7.25 "Florida Sunset," by Harris, 6½" x 16¼". Repeat of title, figs. 7.7 and 7.10.

THIS IS A

Harris Picture

Hand-Painted Water Color

IMPRISONED sunshine, tropical warmth of color, the glow of the sunset skies, the beauty of wind-swept beaches and shifting sand dunes, the shimmer of water on a silver shore—all these are found in HARRIS PICTURES.

Depending first for their success upon the most advanced development of the photographic art, then colored true to nature by skilled artists.

The furnishings of a home show forth the character of the occupants, and nowhere is this more clearly noted than in the pictures. They are an evidence of the appreciation of the finer things, and indicate a love of beauty that finds expression in a charming way.

Those who choose HARRIS PICTURES are safe, for they show discrimination and good taste.

Figure 7.26 "Natural Bridge, Fla.," by Harris, 7½" x 9½". Natural bridge over Arch Creek, Miami.

Figure 7.27 "City Gates, St. Augustine, Florida," by Harris, 6" x 12¼".

Figure 7.28 "Seminole Indian Fishing in the Heart of the Everglades," by E. G. Barnhill, dated 1914, goldtone, uranium dye on glass, 10½" x 13½".

Figure 7.29 Untitled, signed "J.R. Wilcox 1890" by Barnhill, 10" x 12¾".

Figure 7.30 "The Magic Curtain E.G. Barnhill," 6¼" x 13½".

Figure 7.31 "The Sentinel E.G. Barnhill," 6" x 10".

Figure 7.32 Untitled, "E.G. Barnhill," 8" x 10".

Figure 7.33 Untitled, "E.G. Barnhill," 6¼" x 13".

Figure 7.34 Untitled, "E.G. Barnhill," 8" x 10".

Figure 7.35 Untitled, signed "J.R. Wilcox 1890" by Barnhill, 4½" x 13".

Figure 7.36 Untitled, "E.G. Barnhill," 5" x 8".

Figure 7.37 Untitled, signed "J.R. Wilcox" by Barnhill, 10" x 18½".

Figure 7.38 Untitled, signed "J.R. Wilcox, 1890" by Barnhill, 10" x 12".

Orangewood and Mauchline Ware Souvenirs

Among the many attractions that drew tourists to Florida at the turn of the twentieth century were the fruit laden orange groves that covered thousands of acres in north central Florida. In addition to the tasty fruit, orange trees provided a ready supply of hardwood that could be used to make a variety of souvenirs. Orangewood was often used in manufacturing carved alligator keepsakes.

Though many of the wooden souvenirs were similar to their carved counterparts, the decorative approach was markedly different. Instead of using the standard carvings, these orangewood mementos were painted with oranges and orange blossoms or poinsettias. Sometimes a "burnt" or pyrographic decoration was added to the design, creating a pleasing textured surface. Period Osky's catalogues indicate that orangewood was used in making boxes, frames, tie racks, and letter holders.

Smaller souvenirs such as pincushions, hatpin holders, paper cutters, and pitchers are listed in Osky's as well. Some had the town the souvenir would be sold in handwritten in India ink on the wood's surface. Sometimes just "Souvenir of Florida" was added.

These orangewood souvenirs usually are associated with Jacksonville, the production center for most of Florida's orangewood memorabilia. Like the carved canes and keepsakes, orangewood souvenirs were made by local crafts-

Figure 8.1 Orangewood letter holder, hand-painted orange, orange blossoms, leaves, 6" x 8".

men, most likely before World War I. Because of Florida's limited industrial development before the war, orangewood souvenirs represent one of the few postwar antiques that can actually be attributed to Florida and Florida artisans.

Unlike orangewood items, Mauchline ware is one of Florida's scarcer wooden souvenir types. Produced in Mauchline, Scotland, it was made of sycamore wood and decorated with varnished photographic transfers depicting various scenes.

Over the years several decorative styles evolved, but it wasn't until the 1860s that the use of photo transfers began. At that time this style was produced primarily for the English market.

There were finely constructed utilitarian items such as boxes, sewing kits, and assorted desktop accessories, and the carefully varnished wood with the contrasting black photo transfers made charming souvenirs that enjoyed a period of popularity among tourists.

By the late 1880s Mauchline ware was being made for popular resorts in America, including those in Florida. Since most of the scenes on Florida Mauchline ware are of Jacksonville, St. Augustine, and the St. Johns River, it would appear these souvenirs were mostly made ca. 1890–1910, when these two cities and traveling the St. Johns were the most popular destinations.

Mauchline ware was produced from the early nineteenth century until 1933, when the factory was destroyed by fire.

Figure 8.2 Orangewood frame, hand-painted orange, orange blossoms, leaves, 8″ x 10″.

Figure 8.3 Mauchline ware napkin rings: "Spanish Fort and Sea Wall, St. Augustine," 1¼″; "East Coast Railway, Key West Florida," 1¾″.

Figure 8.4 Mauchline ware box, "Ponce de Leon Hotel, St. Augustine, Fla.," 1 ¾" x 2 ¼".

Figure 8.5 Mauchline ware string holder, "Royal Palms, Florida," decorative glass inset on finial, 5"; box, "Ponce de Leon Court, St. Augustine, Fla.," 2" d.

Figure 8.6 Mauchline ware boxes: tr, *"Pitts Island, Lake Worth, Florida";* tl, *"Sea Wall Old Fort in Distance, St. Augustine";* b, *"Ponce de Leon Court, St. Augustine, Fla.," all 1 ¾" h. x 2 ¼" d. x 3 ¾".*

Figure 8.7 Mauchline ware egg box, "City Gates St. Augustine, Fla.," 3 ¼" h.

Figure 8.8 Mauchline ware bank, "A Florida Orange Grove Jacksonville, Fla.," 3"; letter opener, "Palmettos Near Jacksonville, Fla.," 10".

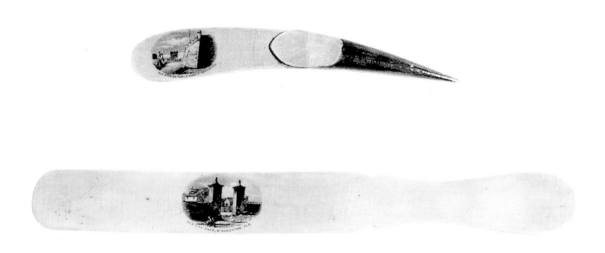

*Figure 8.9 Mauchline ware: letter opener, "Old Spanish Fort and Moat St. Augustine, Fla.";
page flip, "Old City Gates, St. Augustine, Fla."*

Figure 8.10 Orangewood postcard, Osky's cat., ca. 1913.

Figure 8.11 Orangewood pinholder, "Tampa, Fla.," 3″ x 3 ¼″; letter opener, "Sanford, Fla.," 8 ¾″.

Seminole Dolls

One of Florida's most familiar souvenirs is the Seminole Indian doll. These dolls first appeared as souvenirs around 1918 and soon became a favorite with tourists. Few visitors to the Sunshine State returned home without a Seminole doll. They were often purchased as gifts for children, though their rustic native appeal attracted collectors as well. Although some of the earlier dolls were carved from wood, the majority were made with palmetto fiber. They are easily recognized by the colorful banding and patchwork designs that accentuate their clothing.

First conceived as simple toys for Seminole children, the dolls were originally made of cypress or other local woods that could be easily carved. Usually the head and body consisted of a simple whittled cylindrical form with no legs or arms. The dolls were usually clad in calico dresses similar to the clothing worn by the Seminole women at the time. Wooden dolls were made by the men in the tribe, as woodworking was a task customarily reserved for males. Cotton rag dolls, also made about this time, are rare, and most predate the palmetto dolls. Nevertheless, there was a revival of the rag doll types ca. 1930–1940, most of which feature hand sewn cotton cloth bodies, including arms and legs (see fig. 9.10).

Because of constant infringement on their land by white men, the Seminole had lost much of their traditional territory by the 1920s. The loss of hunting grounds and the draining of the Everglades forced some living near the more populated non-Indian areas to adapt to the incursions rather than retreat far-ther into the wilderness. To do this some turned existing camps into cultural exhibitions. By the first decade of the twentieth century tourists could visit the camps at Pine Island in Ft. Lauderdale and Coppinger's Tropical Gardens in Miami, where the Seminole sold handmade "Indian" souvenirs.

Around 1918 the Seminole women at Coppinger's began producing pal-metto fiber dolls to sell to tourists. Fiber was gathered from the trunk of the palmetto palm, allowed to dry, and then cut into flat lengths of two to ten inches, depending on the doll's size. The lengths were then wrapped around a palmetto fiber or cotton filling to finish the body. Heads were made separately and then added to complete the doll form. Male and female dolls are easily distinguished because, unlike the female dolls, male dolls have arms, legs, and feet. Because they were more complicated, fewer male dolls were made.

It appears that earlier dolls were stuffed with the traditional fiber and later dolls with cotton. Usually the body padding can be determined by gently squeezing it. Palmetto fiber feels grainy and rough, while cotton gives evenly. The regular use of cotton filler appears to have started with the revival of tourism following World War II. The subsequent increase in the demand for dolls necessitated the use of cotton, which was readily available and less trouble than palmetto fiber.

Facial features, though often simplistic, sometimes offer a clue to a doll's age. For instance, the eyes and mouths on earlier dolls are smaller and more proportional to the face than on later dolls, whose features seem exaggerated. Also, noses and eyebrows were sometimes added to dolls before ca. 1950. However, as collectors become more experienced, they will find that there are many variables in dating dolls. Familiarity is more valuable than description for deciding a doll's age.

With this in mind, Seminole dolls' hairstyles provide other clues. For the most part, the dolls' hair fashions changed to match those of their makers, about every ten years or so. This continued until the 1960s. Before the 1940s Seminole women wore their hair in buns or rolls. From ca. 1920 to ca. 1930 most doll makers used black wool thread, black material, or horsehair over the head to represent hair (see fig. 9.6). In the early 1930s the women started wearing their hair forward, creating a roll at the top of their foreheads. This was reflected in the dolls' hair as a gentle rise to the top front portion of the head, achieved by using a tight roll of fabric, again covered in black cloth (see fig. 9.7). In the mid- to late 1930s Seminole women began styling their hair around crescent-shaped cardboard forms secured with a hairnet. At first the hair appeared as low semicircular crests, but by the 1940s these had developed into pronounced crescent-shaped halos of hair. This noticeable change was soon adopted by the doll makers and is still popular today (see fig. 9.17). By the late 1960s dolls were beginning to be made with wool braided pigtails or nylon fringe ponytails, again hairstyles currently being worn by the women.

Clothing is also a useful dating reference. Like their hair, the dolls' dress styles were often similar to those of their maker. Female dolls, no matter the age, exhibit a two-piece outfit that includes a full-length dress and loose bodice. Most male dolls wore traditional long shirts, also called "big shirts," that extended to their knees. The male dolls probably appeared about the same time that the female dolls did, that is, ca. 1918.

Fortunately there were subtle yet distinctive changes in banding and patchwork designs that help determine the doll's age, usually within ten to fifteen years. For the most part, male and female dolls share these transitional patterns. The earliest female dolls wore calico dresses with a few areas of intermittent banding. These usually date ca. 1880–ca. 1920 and were made as toys for children.

The first commercial doll dresses, from ca. 1920 to ca. 1930, tended to consist of large single bands of color, bracketed by smaller even-colored stripes. Occasionally one or two bands of calico were used to complete the design (see fig. 9.6). Patchwork first appears about this time. It was usually represented by a single band of two varying colors in simple, repetitive, block-like or triangular designs (see fig. 9.13). In 1933 an Episcopal missionary, Deaconess Harriet M. Bedell, began working among the Seminole. She encouraged their creativity and urged them to produce quality items, which she helped market. Under her supervision doll making and other crafts excelled for nearly twenty years.

From ca. 1930 to ca. 1940 we find two distinct dress designs being used. The most common of the two consisted of four to five alternating bands of color. Though similar to the linear patterned clothing of the previous decade, the dresses and the men's long shirts of this period had a narrower, more uniform banding (see fig. 9.18). The second type is basically the same as the first, with the addition of one or two rows of patchwork (see fig. 9.11). By now the patchwork had become more complex. Repeated letters from the alphabet like S, I, T, Y, and X were common motifs, as well as repeated linear symbols representing trees, turtles, and so on. These designs were usually perpendicular to their borders (see fig. 9.12).

Around the beginning of the 1940s patchwork designs underwent a number of changes. Especially around 1950, new styles and variations on old ones were tilted, creating diagonal courses of sequential themes. As many as three colors were used in a single band (see fig. 9.22). Again, one or two rows of decorative banding were common. By the early 1950s the doll makers started using thin rickrack in addition to the patchwork and alternating color bands.

Often jewelry worn by the dolls is helpful in dating them. Before the 1950s most Seminole doll jewelry consisted of strands of opaque or translucent single-color beads. As many as four colors of beads might be used. These were placed on the doll's neck in an orderly fashion, creating individual bands of color (see fig. 9.3a). After about 1950 the bead colors were usually mixed on the strands (see fig. 9.28).

Earrings started appearing around the 1930s, usually consisting of a single line of three to four beads with a larger round bead at the bottom. On occasion, a short single strand of monochromatic beads was looped and attached to the side of the doll's head to simulate earrings. After ca. 1950 the multicolored beaded loop earring became the norm.

It is important to remember that dating Seminole dolls by their clothing, hair, and jewelry is not a science. Nevertheless, together these features should provide a fairly reliable guideline.

Figure 9.1 Pair of cvd. cypress Seminole dolls, 1935: female, "To: The Otto's," "1935 Bob Barnett," signed in pencil on base, 5⅜"; male, 6".

P. 9.2 Pair of cvd. pine Seminole dolls, ca. 1930–1940: female, 5¾"; male, 6", both signed ARW and MKR (probably stands for maker).

Figure 9.3 Cvd. cypress Seminole doll, ca. 1930, articulated arms with full anatomically correct cvd. body, traditional Seminole blouse and skirt, 10½".

Figure 9.3a Detail of face, Figure 9.3.

Figure 9.4 Cvd. cypress Seminole doll, ca. 1930–1940, articulated arms and undefined cylindrical body, conventional dress, 9".

Figure 9.5 Seminole dolls, ca. 1920–1930: l, Palm fiber body and arms, horsehair hair, attached tag "Hoke-Tee Seminole for woman," 10½"; r, palm fiber body, 13½".

Figure 9.6 Seminole dolls, ca. 1920–1930 (beaded eyes, stitched facial features, rolled palm fiber arms attached to palm fiber bodies indicate dolls made by the same hand), 11¼" and 10½" with horsehair hair.

Figure 9.7 Seminole doll, ca. 1920–1930, palm fiber body, 9¼".

Figure 9.8 Male Seminole rag doll, 1938, 16¼". Old attached tag reads "Seminole Indian Doll, Sent by Mrs. G.L. Molter 1938." The shirt is printed fabric, not patchwork, suggesting a commercial, non-Indian-made doll..

Figure 9.9 Seminole rag doll, ca. 1930–1940, 11″.

Figure 9.10 Seminole rag dolls, ca. 1930–1940, 6¾″ and 9¾″.

Figure 9.11 Seminole doll, ca. 1930–1940, 9¼″.

Figure 9.12 Seminole doll, ca. 1930–1940, 11".

Figure 9.13 Seminole dolls, ca. 1930–1940, both 10½".

Figure 9.14 Male Seminole doll in canoe, ca. 1940–1950: doll, 4"; canoe, 10" and mkd. on base "Hand Carved by Seminole Indians."

Figure 9.15 Male Seminole doll, ca. 1930–1940, 11".

Figure 9.16 Seminole dolls, ca. 1935–1940, 10", 17½", and 9".

Figure 9.17 Seminole doll, ca. 1935–1945, 11".

Figure 9.18 Seminole dolls, ca. 1935–1945: female, 8"; male, 8½", attached tag "From Uncle Lincoln March 1938."

Figure 9.19 Male Seminole dolls, ca. 1935–1945, 10½" and 11".

Figure 9.20 Male Seminole doll, ca. 1935–1945, 15".

Figure 9.21 Seminole dolls, ca. 1940–1950: female, 10½", ca. 1935–1945; male, 10", ca. 1950–1960.

Figure 9.22 Male Seminole doll, ca. 1950–1960, 11½".

Figure 9.23 Palmetto fiber dolls, ca. 1935–1945: female, 6½"; male, 7½". Similar to those made by Seminoles (all palm fiber construction) but decidedly different style: most are not dressed in typical Seminole clothing; those that are have hair bunched and cropped at the top, a style common among Florida Indians depicted by Jacque LeMoyne in 1564, more than 200 years before Seminoles arrived in Florida. Whether variations of the dolls made by Seminoles or commercial copies not yet determined.

Figure 9.24 Palmetto fiber dolls: l, doll labeled "Seminole Indians Brought Here 1941," 13"; r, 12¼".

Figure 9.25 Palmetto fiber dolls, ca. 1930–1940, 12½", 14½", and 11¼".

Figure 9.26 Male Seminole doll, ca. 1940–1950, 9½".

Figure 9.27 Male Seminole dolls, ca. 1950–1960, 8½" and 10".

Figure 9.28 Campaign dolls, 1952–1954, 3¼" and 3½". Courtnay Campbell ran as a democratic congressional candidate in 1952 and won. He ran again in 1954 and lost.

Souvenir Glass

As commercially successful as glass was during the Golden Age, it is surprising that so little is represented among Florida souvenirs.

Glass souvenirs were of two basic types, pressed and blown. Pressed glass was made by pouring molten glass into a mold to create the form. The glass was usually "flashed" or stained ruby red, a method made popular during the Columbian Exposition of 1893. Flashing was a cheap alternative to coloring glass and was not limited to ruby glass. Other colors, such as yellow, green, and white, were used as well. The souvenirs were identified by engraving or etching through the tinted color into the clear glass beneath (see fig. 10.3). This added detail was most likely provided by local jewelers, who often sold the glass. Pressed glass can usually be identified by a visible crease running from the rim to the bottom on either side of the glass.

Another type of pressed glass souvenir was the paperweight. Popular at the beginning of the century, these were usually thick rectangular forms that displayed a Florida scene under glass. Most of the images used in the paperweights were photographic and at times hand tinted to add a touch of color. They retained their popularity until the 1950s.

Blown glass, somewhat more refined than the pressed ware, was usually blown in a mold to achieve the desired shape. Sometimes the surface of the more expensive souvenir glass would be decorated with hand-colored enamel transfers similar to those used on souvenir china. These pieces generally date from the 1890s to ca. 1910 (see fig. 10.5). Others were freely hand painted using white enamel on colored glass. This style is commonly referred to as Mary Gregory glass and was popular from the 1850s to 1900. However, the St. Augustine examples shown in figure 10.6 most likely date from 1885 to ca. 1895.

Finally there is cut glass. This type of decoration was first used in the United States around 1810, reaching its decorative zenith in the Brilliant period around 1880 to 1915. This method involved cutting the desired design onto the glass surface using a foot-powered or electric graver's wheel (see fig. 10.11). Though cut-glass souvenirs are rare, they are among the most elegant of all Florida glass memorabilia.

The informative 1885 advertising section from *The Naturalist in Florida* lists "Engraved Tumblers" described as "bearing engravings of the Fort, City Gates, Yacht Club House, Cathedral, and other places of interest." Though the tumblers were not illustrated, the 1885 periodical gives us a valuable chronological reference.

Glass souvenirs are usually overlooked by Florida collectors, as they are often harder to find than other souvenir types. Still, they are an important part of our Florida history and add a scintillating elegance not found among other souvenirs.

Figure 10.1 St. Augustine vase, 7 ¼"; rose bowl, 4", both mkd. "Old City Gates St. Augustine" and "Austrian" on the base, ca. 1890–1900. Opaque glass decorated with enm. transfers.

Florida's Golden Age of Souvenirs

Figure 10.2 St. Augustine platter, 11 ⅞", hand-painted picture of City Gates in St. Augustine, ca. 1880–1890, Mt. Washington–type glass.

Figure 10.3 Ruby flash glass: tumbler eng. "Sub-Tropical Jacksonville, Fla. Feb. 12th 1891," 3½" (the Sub-Tropical Exposition was held in Jacksonville, 1888–1891); pitcher, eng. "Fla. State Fair, 1906 Louise," 4".

Figure 10.4 Pressed glass souvenirs: "Souvenir of St. Petersburg Fla.," 2½"; "White Springs Fla., Way down upon the Suwanne River," 2½"; "Palm Beach, Florida," 2½", all ca. 1900–1910.

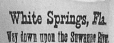

Figure 10.5 Enm. transfer glass: shotglass, "Prize Pineapple from Ft. Pierce, Fla.," 2¼"; tumbler, "The Home of the Orange, Arcadia, Fla.," 4⅜".

Figure 10.6 Mary Gregory glass, "City Gates, St. Augustine, Fla.," ca. 1885–1895, both 4".

Figure 10.7 St. Augustine ruby flash glass, S & P eng. "Sara Buhl St. Augustine, 1903," 3".

Figure 10.8 Daytona ruby flash glass, mug eng. "James H. White Daytona, Fla. 1904 From WLN," 4".

Figure 10.9 Palm Beach creamer, silver overlay, "Palm Beach, Fla.," ca. 1900–1910, 2½".

Figure 10.10 Decanter, Florida scene, detailed engraving of alligator, flowering plants, swamp grass surrounds bottle, ca. 1880–1890, 13½".

Figure 10.11 St. Petersburg tumbler, eng. "St. Petersburg, Fla. 1912, Elva R. Johnson," 5½".

Figure 10.12 Lakeland paperweight, "Passenger Station, Lakeland, Fla.," ca. 1900–1910.

Florida's Golden Age of Souvenirs

Souvenir Jewelry

Because jewelry is rarely associated with the curiosity trade, it is often overlooked by souvenir collectors. Still it was a distinctive part of the souvenir business and offers the collector an elegant array of intricate treasures.

During the Golden Age many of the souvenir shops stocked jewelry with Florida motifs. Jewelry appealed not only to women but to men as well. Women enjoyed a wide selection of breast pins, brooches, pendants, and the like, while men found a variety of cufflinks, watch fobs, and tie pins. Carved alligator pins and enameled silver brooches with the crest of St. Augustine were particularly popular. It was a curious mix of machine made and handmade jewelry. Like spoons, the majority of silver jewelry came from New England metal smiths, while most of the alligator ornaments were made by carvers in Jacksonville. Fortunately this techno-contrast resulted in a refreshing array of souvenir jewelry that tastefully celebrated Florida's historical heritage and untamed wilderness.

Florida's first jewelry related souvenirs were most likely simple bangles made from available shells or alligator teeth. Fish scale jewelry is documented in Webb's Jacksonville Directories by the early 1870s but actually pre-dates the Civil War. This type of jewelry remained popular until after the turn of the century and was made from the scales of garfish, tarpon, and other similar fish. The delicate nature of fish scale jewelry makes it quite rare.

The 1876 and 1886 issues of Webb's mentions Anthony Boden of Jacksonville as an alligator tooth polisher. Primarily used for jewelry such as breast pins, bracelets, and the like, many of the teeth were supplied by the Seminole hunters from South Florida.

The 1885 tourist edition of *The Naturalist in Florida* refers to a variety of adornments offered by the Fort Marion store in St. Augustine. As could be expected, much of the jewelry was fashioned from alligator teeth. Items offered included single or double alligator tooth veil pins, cuff buttons, watch charms, scarf pins, and eardrops, all in "solid gold" settings.

An assortment of sea bean jewelry was listed as well. These pieces consisted of a variety of red sea bean charms, scarf pins, eardrops, brooches, watch fobs, and bracelets, with some of the bracelets made of a combination of sea beans and alligator teeth. Some of the sea bean charms and watch fobs were engraved or inset with a small compass. One type is described as "set with microscopic views of the City Gates, Cathedral, St. Francis Street and Fort Marion." Today such items are referred to as stanhopes. A stanhope is typically a minute black-and-white negative image covered by a small magnifier that when held to the light enlarges the views. Stanhopes were placed in a variety of American souvenirs but are extremely rare in those from Florida.

Another form of jewelry sold at the Ft. Marion store included necklaces, neck collars, and bracelets made of pearl shell. These were interlaced shells knotted in macramé to best exhibit the shells' lustrous beauty. Fish scale jewelry was carried as well. Items like brooches, earrings, hair ornaments, and necklaces were offered and listed as "made from the scales of fish caught in Florida waters."

By the early 1900s Osky's Curios and Novelties of Jacksonville offered a variety of alligator tooth jewelry, either plain or sporting a carved alligator. Osky's also advertised a line of handmade abalone jewelry. Among the most unusual offerings were sterling settings featuring "Brazelean" (Brazilian) beetles (see fig. 11.28). Their hard luminescent green shells were mounted on hatpins, bracelets, stickpins, and cufflinks. Osky's also offered necklaces and bracelets made from coffee shell, coral, turquoise, amber, and even Spanish bayonet seeds.

Besides their "natural" jewelry line, Osky's advertised a limited selection of "cloisonné jewelry," which was actually made using the champlevé technique (see p. 75, c). Most of the jewelry featured enameled oranges or poinsettias. Greenleaf and Crosby also carried champlevé jewelry, as well as a die-stamped and die-cut selection (see fig. 11.5t) Like spoons, these last two decorative techniques could be enhanced with enameling or gold wash. Greenleaf and Crosby have advertised as jewelers since 1868 and probably made some of the jewelry themselves. Given the company's longevity and the size of the business, it is likely that many new discoveries of this firm's creations await those interested in Florida jewelry.

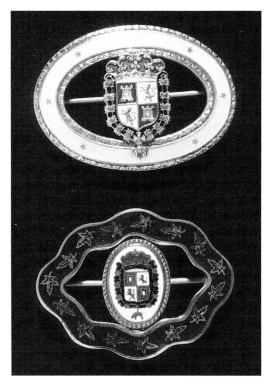

Figure 11.1 St. Augustine, "City Gates, Fla.," sterling enm. brooch, 2".

Figure 11.2 Florida sterling enm. brooch, "Great Seal of Florida In God We Trust," 2 ¾".

Figure 11.3 Orange and orange blossom sterling brooches: tl, 2 ⅛"; tr, 2 ¼"; b, 2".

Figure 11.4 Sterling enm. Spanish crest pins, both 2 ⅛".

Figure 11.5 Sterling enm. alligator pins: t, 1 ¾"; c, 2 ⅜"; b, "Florida," 1 ⁹⁄₁₆".

Figure 11.6 Sterling enm. poinsettia pins: t, 1¼"; cl, 1/16"
G&C cat., ca. 1900–1910; cr, 1/2"; b, 2⅛" bar pin.

Figure 11.7 Sterling enm. Spanish crest pins: t, 1½"; b, "St.
Augustine Florida Founded 1565," 1¹/₁₆".

Figure 11.8 Sterling state seal pins, 1⅜" and 2".

Figure 11.9 Sterling enm. bar pins, 2¼"–3¼".

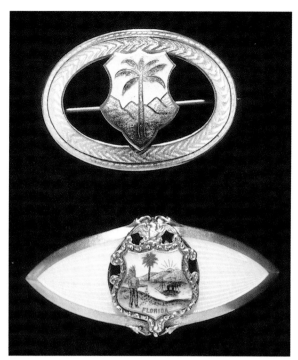

Figure 11.10 Sterling enm. Florida pins: t, 1 ¾", G&C cat., ca. 1905; b, Florida state seal, 2½".

Figure 11.11 Enm. "Florida" pins: t, sterling, ¹¹/₁₆"; bl, brass, ¾"; br, brass, ⅞".

Figure 11.12 Sterling enm. orange and orange blossom pins, 1", G&C cat., ca. 1905, and 2½".

Figure 11.13 Sterling enm. seal pins: "Great Seal of the State of Florida In God We Trust," 2 ¼"; "Key West, Florida" around seal of Key West, 2 ⅛".

Figure 11.14 Sterling enm. bar pins, 1 1/16"–1 3/4".

Figure 11.15 Sterling enm. Spanish crest pins: t, 1½"; c, 2½"; b, 1 3/8".

Figure 11.16 G&C cat. illustration of selection of sterling champlevé jewelry, ca. 1900–1910.

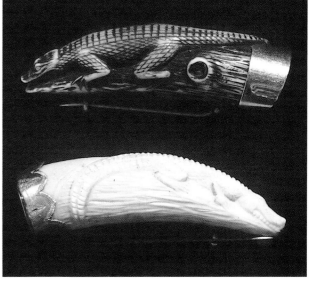

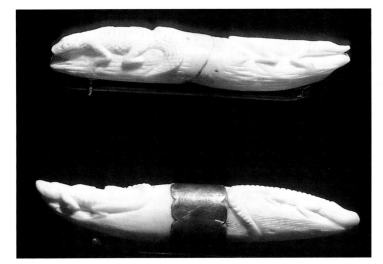

Figure 11.17 Jeweler's business card featuring alligator tooth jewelry; Mackey was in business from 1881 to 1892.

Figure 11.18 Cvd. alligator tooth brooches, stained for contrast, gold cap, 2½".

Figure 11.19 Twin cvd. alligator tooth brooches, 2½" and 2⅛".

Figure 11.20 Cvd. alligator tooth brooches, 2¼" and 2½".

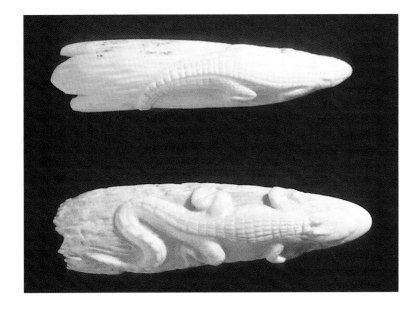

Figure 11.21 Cvd. alligator brooches: t, *ivory, 2½"*; c, *bone, 1½"*; b, *ivory, 2".*

Figure 11.22 Double alligator tooth pin, "E. R. Palatka, Fla. 1893" eng. on gold band, 2¾", possibly made by Charles Warren of Palatka, who advertised making "alligator tooth jewelry" around this time.

Figure 11.23 Florida motif cufflinks.

Figure 11.24 Sterling Spanish crest belt buckles: tl, 2½", G&C cat.; tr, 3"; b, 1½".

Figure 11.25 Large sterling Spanish crest pin, 2¼".

Figure 11.26 Sterling Florida motif stickpins.

Figure 11.27 Stickpins: cvd. ivory alligator; sterling alligator.

Figure 11.28 "Brazelean" beetle brooch and stickpin, Osky's cat., ca. 1913.

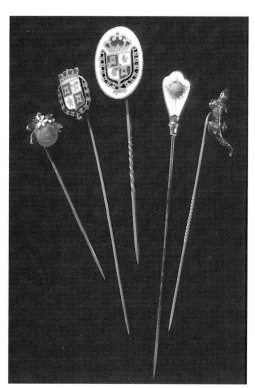

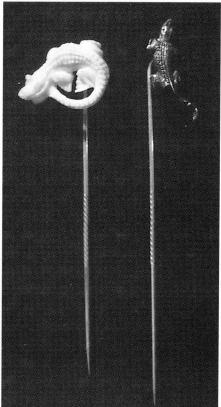

Figure 11.29 Sterling bracelet, emb. "St. Augustine, Florida."

Figure 11.30 Brass buckle and brooch: buckle, ca. 1890–1900, 2⅛"; brooch with green glass cabochon, 1925–1935, 2¾".

Figure 11.31 Enm. Florida scenes on sterling: t, 1"; bl, ⅞"; br, ⅞". Bottom pins are hand-painted enm. rather than typical champlevé.

Figure 11.32 Hand-painted porcelain pins, ca. 1920–1930, pin at right has embossed oranges, both 1¼".

Figure 11.33 Porcelain pins, ca. 1920–1930, all hand-colored transfer decal images, 1 ⅛"–1 ¼".

Figure 11.34 Glass pins, ca. 1930–1940, mounted on sterling, both ¾".

Figure 11.35 "Gasparilla" souvenir pins: l, "Souvenir Gasparilla Carnival and South Florida Fair Feb. 4–12 1916," brass, 1 ¾"; tr, "Tampa, Fla.," sterling, ca. 1904–1910, ¾"; br, "South Florida Fair, Gasparilla Jan. 29–Feb. 9 1929," celluloid, ⅞". The Gasparilla carnival and fair began in 1904 and are still annual events.

Figure 11.36 Florida pins and fob: tl, "Old Gates St. Augustine, 1"; tr, fob state seal "In God We Trust"; cl, Florida state seal "In God We Trust"; cr, oranges and "Florida"; b, orange blossoms. Top four are enm. on brass, ½"–1 ¼".

Figure 11.37 Brass pins: t, "Orlando Florida 1923," 1¾"; b, "Florida" featuring St. Augustine, City Gates, in relief, ca. 1900–1910.

Figure 11.38 Watch fobs: t, "Florida The Summerland," white metal, ca. 1920–1930, 1"; bl, white metal, ca. 1900–1910, 1½"; br, "Florida," white metal, ca. 1920–1930, 1½".

Figure 11.39 Camp Cuba Libre souvenirs: l, "Gen. Fitzhugh Lee com'd 7th Corps.," reverse, "1895 Camp Cuba Libre Jacksonville, Fla."; r, first bar "Camp Cuba Libre," second bar "Jacksonville, Fla.," medal "Honor to Our Country's Brave." Both are brass (see Figure 5.50).

Figure 11.40 Pins and stanhope: l, "Capitol, Tallahassee, Fla.," eng. sterling; c, Stetson, Deland celluloid stick pin; r, turned ivory stanhope views, St. Augustine, "New and Old, Cathedral, City Gates, Oldest House, Old Slave Market, Alcazar Hotel, Ponce de Leon Hotel," all ca. 1895–1905.

Olive Commons Jewelry and Porcelain

A book on Florida souvenirs would not be complete without a chapter on Olive Commons. She was a gifted china painter whose busy hands crafted some of Florida's most beautiful souvenirs.

Born Olive Wesler on June 8, 1880, in Richmond, Indiana, Olive showed an early interest in art. By high school she was focusing on art related classes, and, encouraged by her parents, took private lessons to further refine her skills.

At the age of twenty Olive married Arthur B. Commons, also a resident of Richmond. With his support she continued her artistic pursuits and began china painting. Before long she joined the local art clubs and became one of the more respected artists in her community.

In 1908 Olive and Arthur moved to a remote central Florida town called Mossdale. Now a ghost town, it was located between Deland and Sanford, near the St. Johns River. According to local legend Arthur was hired to manage an orange grove in the area. Soon the couple found the perfect island home on the St. Johns, which offered an incomparable panoramic view of the river. Stately palms and moss-draped oaks lined the surrounding shores. Local orange groves were fragrant and flush with golden fruit.

Inspired by the ethereal beauty of her environs, Olive started working on her ceramics. She began painting small riverscapes on porcelain medallions, mounting them as jewelry and giving them to friends as Christmas gifts. Each piece was carefully painted, placed in her kiln, and fired to 1800 degrees to bind the enamel paint to the porcelain form. The St. Johns seemed to flow from her tiny brushes.

The natural charm of the jewelry she called "cameonas" soon gained them popularity among locals and tourists as well. Realizing the potential market for her jewelry, Olive, with Arthur's encouragement, began selling her "cameonas" to local tourist shops in Deland and Sanford.

In 1922 she advertised in the *Florida Grower*, stating that the "cameonas" were "Florida's most sought after gift, at once typical, useful, ornamental and practically indestructible." Besides the popular river scenes she also carried brooches and pins featuring colorful oranges, orange blossoms, and other flowers, including poinsettias.

Stimulated by the local success of the business the Commons family decided to move to Miami in 1924. Here a booming tourist economy assured a much larger clientele. The couple settled in Coconut Grove, where Olive opened her new studio and Arthur handled the advertising. They called the shop the House of Commons.

It was here that she developed the delightful line of hand-painted dinnerware she called "platinum palm ware." As the name suggests, a special platinum glaze was used to create her silver landscapes. The lustrous designs produced a pleasing contrast to the pure white background of the china and did not tarnish.

Olive began decorating the porcelain tableware with palms, moss laden oaks, palmettos, and other typical Florida scenery. These "palm ware" designs were applied to her jewelry as well (see fig. 12.14). Sometimes the palm ware images were reversed so that the platinum dominated the background.

No matter the format, her new silvery designs captured the heart of the Florida wilds, and the heart of the tourist as well. In 1939 she displayed her decorated china at the New York World's Fair, where she won the Highest Award of Merit medal for her "platinum palm ware" designs.

She introduced another line of porcelain jewelry, using black enamel to create her motifs. These were rather simple designs and usually featured a galleon or palm tree (see fig. 12.16). This line was probably some of her later work, possibly made between 1940 and 1950.

Olive continued making her original polychrome cameona jewelry but apparently never produced any similar dinnerware. She signed most of her color cameonas using her initials, a simple *O* superimposed on the letter *C*. Her signature usually appears near the bottom of the cameona and is often inconspicuous, hidden in the water or foliage of the design.

She chose not to sign her platinum jewelry but did mark her larger dinnerware pieces on the back. Some have a simple "Commons, Miami" hand painted in the platinum glaze. Others are marked with a commercial stamp that reads "Platinum Palm-Ware Commons Miami."

Though she sold her porcelains worldwide, Olive kept her quaint cottage industry self-contained. She sketched and developed her own designs, painted them by hand, and fired them in a kiln on her back porch. Arthur's death in 1945 left Olive to carry on the business alone. A determined woman however, she prevailed, and the House of Commons continued its successful course until her death in 1963.

Throughout her life, Olive Commons was a dedicated artist. Her evident love for Florida is reflected in her work. Her painted porcelains, both rustic and refined, invite the viewer to pause and bask in the serenity of sunset solitude or the shimmering hollow of a platinum hammock. Olive's talent for capturing the essence of the St. Johns River and the tropical wilds of South Florida is legendary. Her exquisite landscapes caught the remnant soul of an undeveloped paradise on the crest of change.

Figure 12.1 Cameona pins: l, 2³⁄₁₆"; c, 2¼"; r, 2⅛".

Figure 12.2 Oversized cameona porcelain, 5⅜", with frame 6½". Extraordinary size indicates Olive's polychrome landscapes were not confined to jewelry.

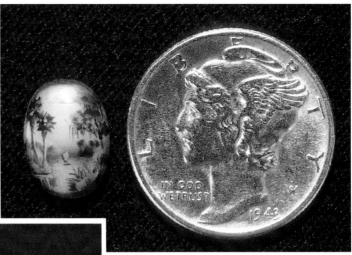

Figure 12.3 Small unmounted cameona, ⅜", illustrates Olive's gift for detail.

Figure 12.4 Cameonas, pins and pendants, ⅞"–1¼".

Figure 12.5 Orange blossom cameonas: c, 2¹/₁₆".

Figure 12.6 Poinsettia cameonas: l, 2³/₁₆"; tr, 1½"; br, 1³/₁₆".

Figure 12.7 River palm cameonas, 2" and 2¼".

Figure 12.8 Bar pins: t, 1½"; c, 2"; l, 1½".

CAMEONA
Painted by
Mrs. A. B. Commons
Miami, Fla.

CAMEONA
Painted by
Mrs. A. B. Commons
Coconut Grove, Fla.

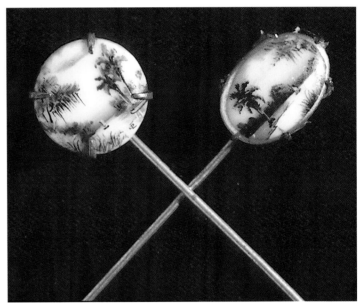

Figure 12.9 Bar pins, 1½"– 2".

Figure 12.10 Cameona card mounts: t, "Miami, Fla."; c, "Coconut Grove, Fla."; b, "Sanford, Fla."

Figure 12.11 Stick pins, ½" and ⅝".

Ref.
17

CAMEONA
Painted by
Mrs. A. B. Commons
Sanford, Fla.

Florida's Golden Age of Souvenirs

Figure 12.12 *Cameona pins: l, 1⅛" x 1⅜"; c, 1¼"; r, 1⅛" x 1⅜".*

Figure 12.13 *Gold palm ware pins: t, ¾" x 1"; b, ½" x 1". Olive decorated most of her palm ware jewelry with a platinum overglaze; here she must have experimented with gold.*

Figure 12.14 *Platinum palm ware pins, 1¹/₁₆"–1¼".*

Figure 12.15 Palm ware pin, 1 ⅜".

Figure 12.16 Palm ware and galleon pins, ca. 1940–1950, all ¾" x 1".

Figure 12.17 Platinum palm ware tea set, each piece signed "Commons, Miami."

Florida's Golden Age of Souvenirs

Figure 12.18 Palm ware S & Ps, 6"; card holder, 2 ¾" x 3 ⅝", all mkd. "Olive Commons."

Figure 12.19 Palm ware candy dish, "Olive Commons" on base, 8½".

Figure 12.20 *Palm ware bowl, 1" high, 4½" d., mkd. "Olive Commons."*

Figure 12.21 *Palm ware dish signed "Olive Commons," 5 ¾" x 5 ¾".*

Figure 12.22 *Palm ware vase signed "Olive Commons," 5" x 4".*

Figure 12.23 Mahogany jar with cameona inset on top, 3" d. x 4¾".

Figure 12.24 Palm ware dish signed "Commons Miami," 4¾" x 4¾".

Silver Springs Pottery

Over the forty years of Florida's Golden Age, only a few art potters opened studios in Florida. Of these only one, Henry Andreas Graack, would remain successful for any length of time.

Graack came to America in 1919 from Denmark, where he had learned to make pottery from his father. He first settled in New York but came to Bradenton, Florida, in 1921 after his father, Henry Andreas Sr., purchased the studio of local art potter Mary Ward. Graack Sr. initially had intended to start a father-son pottery.

Most of the pieces produced at the Bradenton studio were bisque fired. The Graacks decorated the pottery's unglazed surfaces with hand-painted tropical scenery, like palms, parrots, pine trees, and Florida flowers. For the most part the pieces were utilitarian, including vases, ashtrays, and wall pockets. Much of the pottery can be identified by a circular mark stamped on the base that reads "The H.A. Graack & Son Art Pottery, Bradentown, Fla."

Despite the Graacks' best efforts, the Bradenton pottery proved unsuccessful, and production ceased by 1923. The senior Graack went back to Denmark, while Henry returned to New York. Though intent on opening another pottery, he was forced during the next few years to supplement his income working in a brickyard.

In the early 1930s Henry Graack was invited to be the resident potter at Ft. Ticonderoga, New York. Owner Stephen Bell wanted Graack to duplicate Indian pottery found in the region. This location proved to be a good outlet for Graack's pottery though only on a seasonal basis.

He continued working at Ft. Ticonderoga during the summer but needed a winter locale to complete his season. Around 1934 or 1935, he returned to Florida and opened a studio at the popular tourist attraction Silver Springs.

Once he set up his studio, he began experimenting with different low-fired clay bodies, glazes, and forms. He may have developed his familiar three-color swirl pottery here, though examples bearing his Ft. Ticonderoga mark are fairly common. To produce the desired effect he colored two batches of clay, one green, one russet, using mineral oxides. These in turn were mixed with the natural-colored clay. After the pots were made, they were bisque fired. This style of "tourist" pottery proved extremely successful and became the mainstay of Graak's business. The pieces were usually signed "SILVER SPRINGS, FLA." and sold for fifty cents to one dollar.

In some instances Graak chose glazes rather than colored clays for decoration. Existing examples suggest that at least two types of glazes were being used. One produced a unique polychrome effect, consisting of two to four variegated colors that swirled and ran together (see fig. 13.5). Most of these pots have Graack's name either written or stippled on the base. The second glaze was an even matte color, usually blue.

The entry of the United States into World War II in 1941 drastically reduced Florida tourism, leaving Graack no choice but to close for the duration of the war. He used this time expanding his skills as a potter. He visited the potting centers of Zanesville, Ohio, where he learned to make molds to help increase production when he began potting again. Following the war he reopened and introduced his molded ware and the matte glazes. The forms strongly resemble pieces produced at the Roseville Pottery in Zanesville and may suggest that he interned there (see fig. 13.7). His Florida examples were marked with his typical "SILVER SPRINGS, FLA." stamp.

Graack continued his summer visits to his Ft. Ticonderoga studio, following the seasonal trail of the tourist. As a rule, he made the same type of pottery in New York that he did in Florida, the only difference being the mark "FORT TICONDEROGA."

Graack remained an active potter until 1965, when he died after a short illness. The pottery continued for a few more years in the hands of a local potter, Stell Phillips.

Though Graack and his pottery extend beyond the bounds of the Golden Age, it is important to identify all aspects of his artwork. This is especially true when one considers his forty-three years as an exceedingly productive Florida potter.

1293 Green Henson

Greetings From Florida

THIS POTTERY IS SCENTED WITH

Orange Bossom

IT IS MADE BY HAND ON THE POTTER'S
WHEEL FROM FLORIDA CLAYS

AT

SILVER SPRINGS POTTERY

SILVER SPRINGS, FLORIDA

GIFT SENT BY

_____

POTTER: H. A. GRAACK
Assistant Potter: MADELYN GRAACK

Figure 13.1 Graack gift card.

Figure 13.2 Vase with ring-shaped han. stamped "SILVER SPRINGS, FLA.," 8¾", ca. 1935–1945.

Figure 13.3 Glazed creamer and vase: "H.A. Graack, Potter" incised on base with typical "SILVER SPRINGS, FLA." stamp, 4¼"; "Graack" stippled on base and "SILVER SPRINGS, FLA." stamp, 4¼", ca. 1935–1945.

Figure 13.4 Pansy pitchers, rope han.: l, 4¼"; r, 4", both stamped "SILVER SPRINGS, FLA.," ca. 1935–1945. Made to hold flowers that grew around the springs.

Figure 13.5 Glazed pitcher and creamer, rope han.: l, stamped "SILVER SPRINGS, FLA." with "Graack" stippled on base; r, stamped "SILVER SPRINGS, FLA." and incised "Potter H.R. Graack," 3¼", ca. 1935–1945.

Figure 13.6 Glazed vase and jar: vase stamped "SILVER SPRINGS, FLA." with "Graack" incised on base, 4"; jar stamped "SILVER SPRINGS, FLA.," 3", ca. 1935–1945.

Figure 13.7 Blue glazed vases, 3¼" and 4½" x 6", both stamped "SILVER SPRINGS, FLA.," ca. 1945–1955. Both show Roseville influence in shape and color.

Florida's Golden Age of Souvenirs

Figure 13.8 Blue glaze pansy pitcher stamped "SILVER SPRINGS, FLA.," 6½", ca. 1945–1955.

Figure 13.9 Vases: l, 6½"; c, 7⅛"; r, 4½", all stamped "SILVER SPRINGS, FLA.." This group and the following four pictures typify pottery made at Graack's Silver Springs shop from 1935 to 1966.

Figure 13.10 Fan vase and creamer: vase 4¼" x 7¾"; creamer 3⅛" with rope han., both stamped "SILVER SPRINGS, FLA.."

Figure 13.11 Wall pockets: l, mkd. on b. in pencil $1.50 and "From Dad 11/12/48," 4½"; r, 2⅞" h. x 3¾", both stamped "SILVER SPRINGS, FLA."

Figure 13.12 Vases: l, 4"; c, 5⅛"; r, 3¾", *all stamped "SILVER SPRINGS, FLA."*

Figure 13.13 Typical Graack pottery, 2½"–4½".

Metal and Shieldware Souvenirs

Metal souvenirs offer the collector a good variety of Florida memorabilia. They occur as early as the 1890s, most of them imported from Germany. By the end of World War I, German imports were reduced to a trickle, and shop owners turned to Japanese, English, and American manufacturers for their metal souvenirs. It would be the Japanese who would ultimately dominate the production of this type of souvenir.

Little has been written on metal souvenirs, so much of what I offer here is based on a few dated pieces, a couple of identifiable trademarks, and information I have been able to glean from period catalogues.

Before World War I metal souvenirs were usually made with finer alloys than those used after the war. A 1908 Greenleaf and Crosby catalogue advertised fine French and Viennese bronze figurines and statues, as well as full-figure alligator inkwells made of brass, and gator match safes and doorstops of oxidized nickel.

Most of these pieces were either molded or die stamped. Molds were used for the more complicated three-dimensional souvenirs. These included figurines of alligators, pelicans, fish, and the like. Usually a simple two-piece mold was used to make the casting. Die-stamped souvenirs such as plates, ashtrays, and tumblers were made from positive and negative steel plates engraved with the desired Florida motif. The metal form was placed between two plates, which were forced together, impressing the image into the soft metal. Sometimes the two manufacturing techniques were combined. This was common for shieldware items where the figure was cast and the applied shield die stamped.

World War I created a shortage of metals and marked the end of bronze, brass, and nickel souvenirs. These better-grade alloys were replaced by much cheaper pot metal made from a combination of 20 percent lead and 80 percent copper, most of it imported from Japan.

Although some pot metal souvenirs were produced in the late 1910s and 1920s, the type became much more common after the Depression of 1929. They replaced the more expensive Golden Age souvenirs as the growing middle class became more mobile and the wealthy recovered from the Depression. By the early 1930s the industrious Japanese were dominating the souvenir trade with their inexpensive goods, including pot metal mementos. This continued to be the case until World War II abruptly ended U.S. trade with Japan.

Figure 14.1 Match safes: l, *brass "City Gates, St. Augustine, Fla.," b. "Old Fort Marion, St. Augustine, Fla.";* r, *sterling full-figure alligator; G&C cat., ca. 1900–1910.*

Figure 14.2 Match safes: l, *sterling embossed alligator;* c, *snakeskin with brass cartouche, "City Gates," St. Augustine, Fla.;* r, *sterling engraved "St. Augustine," reverse engraved "H.M. Bair, Lancaster, Pa."*

Figure 14.3 Match safes: t, brass "El Telegrafo, Key West," shaped like a cigar box; b, white metal and colored celluloid panels, "West Bay Street, Jacksonville, Fla.," reverse "Hemming Park, Jacksonville."

Figure 14.4 Match safes, alligator leather, Osky's cat., ca. 1905–1915.

Figure 14.5 Matchbook holder and compacts: tl, matchbook holder, "Miami Beach, Fla."; tr, compact, "Miami"; b, compact, "Oldest School House, St. Augustine, Fla.," all ca. 1910–1920.

Figure 14.6 Enm. Spanish crest tray, brass, ca. 1900–1910, 3" x 4".

Figure 14.7 Art nouveau tray, "The Royal Poinciana, Palm Beach, Fla.," pot metal, ca. 1900–1910, 4½" x 10".

Figure 14.8 Plates, pot metal: scenes, clockwise, "Spanish Coat of Arms, Old Fort Marion, Old City Gates, Slave Market, Alcazar Hotel," banner "Souvenir of St. Augustine, Fla.," 4¾"; "Court House and Armory, City Water Works, Elk's Club New Post Office Building, Library and First Presbyterian Church, Windsor Hotel," emb. near base "Souvenir of Jacksonville, Fla.," 7".

Figure 14.9 Tumblers, pot metal: St. Augustine scenes, l to r, "The Alcazar, City Gates, Fort Marion," 2¼"; Tampa scenes, l to r, "Palm Avenue, Tampa Bay Hotel Grounds, A Fine Bunch of Fruit, Tampa Bay Hotel, Post Office and Customs House, 3¼", both ca. 1900–1910.

Figure 14.10 Shieldware box, Tampa, white metal, "Tampa Bay Hotel, Tampa, Fla.," 2½" d. x 2¾" h., ca. 1900–1910.

Figure 14.11 Pocket knives, t and b, aluminum; c, sterling silver switch blade, El Unico cat. 1898, also sold by G&C.

Figure 14.12 Pocket knives, aluminum, ca. 1900–1910.

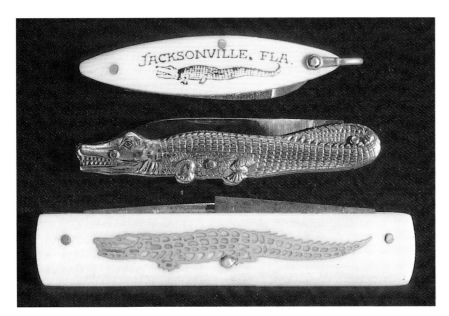

Figure 14.13 Alligator knives: celluloid han., "Jacksonville, Fla."; white metal han., emb. alligator; celluloid han., intaglio gator, all ca. 1910–1920.

Figure 14.14 Straight razor, celluloid han., emb. alligator, ca. 1900–1910.

Figure 14.15 Alligator inkwell, oxidized nickel mkd. "G&C" on base, 8″, ca. 1900–1910.

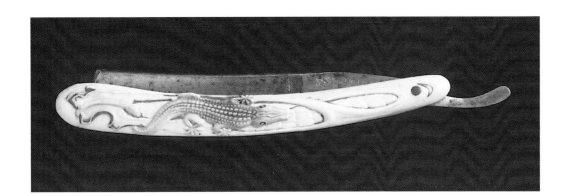

Figure 14.16 Cast iron door stop, 9", ca. 1910–1920.

Figure 14.17 Cane han., brass, ca. 1910–1920, 5". Metal copy of cane type in figure 6.14.

Figure 14.18 Shieldware alligator band, ca. 1915–1925, 2¾"–3½" tall.

Figure 14.19 Napkin rings: l, *1¾" x 3⅝"; r, "Daytona, Fla.," 2½" x 3¾", both ca. 1910–1920.*

Figure 14.20 Figural inkwell, painted pot metal, gator is 4"; stump is 1¾", ca. 1915–1925.

Figure 14.21 Nutcrackers: t, *alligator "Miami, Fla.," 8¾"; l, pelican round shield "Miami Beach, Fla.," 7½"; r, alligator on log, 8", no shield, all ca. 1920–1930.*

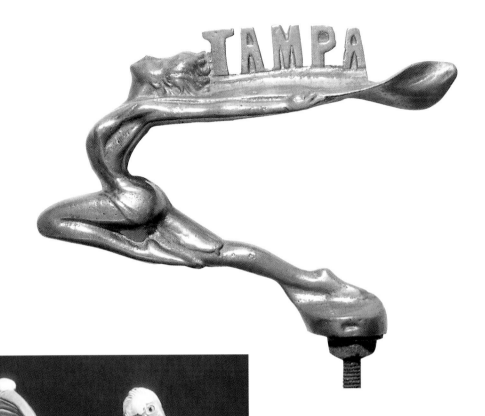

Figure 14.22 Tampa brass hood ornament, ca. 1910–1920, 6½″ x 4½″.

Figure 14.23 Shieldware painted metal pelicans: l, "Palm Beach, Fla.," ca. 1930–1940, 3¾″; r, "St. Petersburg, Fla.," ca. 1920–1930, 4″.

Figure 14.24 Shieldware pelicans: l, copper-washed pot metal; r, painted pot metal, both read "St. Petersburg," 2″, ca. 1920–1930.

Figure 14.25 Shieldware pelicans: l, *"St. Petersburg," ca. 1920–1930, 2"; S and Ps, ca. 1930–1940, 3"; r, "St. Petersburg," ca. 1930–1940, 2".*

Figure 14.26 Shieldware pelican ashtray; 3" h., "Silver Springs, Fla.," ca. 1930–1940.

Figure 14.27 Flamingos, painted pot metal: l, *"Sarasota, Fla.," 4½"; r, 4⅛", both ca. 1930–1940.*

Figure 14.28 Shieldware bulldogs: l, *"Safety Harbor, Fla.," 2"*; r, *"Tampa, Fla.," 3"*, *both ca. 1910–1920.*

Figure 14.29 Shieldware dogs, l to r: *"Silver Springs, Fla.," ca. 1930–1940; "Sarasota, Fla.," ca. 1930–1940; "Florida," ca. 1920–1930; "St. Augustine, Fla.," ca. 1910–1920; "Miami, Fla.," ca. 1910–1920, size range 2"–3 ¼".*

Figure 14.30 Shieldware figures: l, Indian, "Palm Beach, Fla.," 3½", ca. 1920–1930; r, tank, "St. Petersburg, Fla.," 3", ca. 1920–1930.

Figure 14.31 Change purse, "City Gates, St. Augustine," ca. 1900–1910, 3" d, white metal top, bag of silver-colored German cut-steel beads.

Figure 14.32 Shieldware: collapsible shoehorn, "St. Petersburg, Fla.," open, 4¾"; bookmark, "Miami," 2⅛", both ca. 1910–1920.

Figure 14.33 Frame, pot metal, "Souvenir of Florida," 3" x 4", 1920–1930.

Bibliography

Barbour, George M. 1884. *Florida for Tourists, Invalids, and Settlers*. New York: Appleton.

Bednersh, Wayne. 1998. *Collectible Souvenir Spoons, Identification and Values*. Paducah, Ky.: Collector Books.

Bell, Jeanenne. 1991. *Answers to Questions about Old Jewelry, 1840 to 1950*. Florence, Ala.: Books America.

Blackard, David M. 1990. *Patchwork and Palmettos*. Ft. Lauderdale: Historical Museum.

Booker, George E. 1992. *Jacksonville Riverport*. Columbia: University of South Carolina Press.

Brinton, Daniel. 1869 [1978]. *Guide Book of Florida and the South*. Gainesville: University Presses of Florida.

Brown, Paul. 1895. *The Book of Jacksonville, A History*. Poughkeepsie, N.Y.: A. V. Height.

Burgess, Arene. 1996. *A Collector's Guide to Souvenir Plates*. Atglen, Pa.: Schiffer.

Caron, Jonathan F. 1992. *American Souvenir Teaspoon Handbook*. Dover, N.H.: Odyssey Press.

Chandler, David Leon. 1986. *Henry Flagler*. New York: Macmillan.

Congdon-Martin, Douglas. 1994. *Figurative Cast Iron, A Collectors Guide*. Atglen, Pa.: Schiffer.

Cushing, Monroe D. 1883. *Florida State Gazetteer and Business Directory, 1883–84*. Jacksonville: Cushing and Appleyard.

Davidson, James Wood. 1889. *The Florida of Today*. New York: Appleton.

Davis, Frederick. 1925. *History of Jacksonville, Florida, and Vicinity*. St. Augustine: Record Company.

Dewhurst, William W. 1881. *St. Augustine, Florida*. New York: G. Putnam.

Directory of St. Augustine. Vol. 1. New York: Interstate Directory, 1899.

Downs, Dorothy. 1995. *Art of the Florida Seminole and Miccosukee Indians*. Gainesville: University Press of Florida.

Esgate, James. 1885. *Jacksonville, The Metropolis of Florida*. Boston: Wm. G. J. Perry.

Florida 23: The Journal of Decorative and Propaganda Arts, 1875–1945. Miami: Wolfsonian at Florida International University, 1998.

Fox, Charles Donald. 1925. *The Truth about Florida*. New York: Charles Regard.

Frankel, Alfred R. 1999. *Old Florida Pottery*. St. Petersburg: Blue Dome Press.

Gannon, Michael. 1993. *Florida: A Short History*. Gainesville: University Press of Florida.

Garbarino, Merwyn S. 1989. *Indians of North America: The Seminole*. New York: Chelsea House.

Glasgow, Vaughn L. 1991. *A Social History of the American Alligator*. New York: St. Martins Press.

Gold, Daniel Pleasant. 1928. *History of Duval County, Florida*. St. Augustine: Record Company.

Goller, Robert R. 1991. "The North and South with W. J. Harris, Photographer." *El Escribano* 28 (St. Augustine Historical Society).

Henshall, James A. 1884. *Camping and Cruising in Florida*. Cincinnati: Robert Clark.

History Guide and Directory, St. Augustine, Florida. 1904. St. Augustine: St. Augustine Record.

Ingram, H. K. 1895–1896. *Tourist and Settler's Guide to Florida*. Jacksonville: DaCosta.

Jacksonville City Directory and Business Advertiser for 1871. Jacksonville: Florida Union Book and Job Office.

Jacksonville City Directory for 1870. Jacksonville: Florida Union Book and Job Office.

Johnson, Clifton. 1918. *Highways and Byways of Florida*. New York: Macmillan.

Julian, Ralph. 1895. *Dixie: Or Southern Scenes and Sketches*. New York: Harper and Bros.

Lanier, Sidney, 1876. *Florida: Its Scenery, Climate, and History*. Philadelphia: J. B. Lippincott.

Ledyard, Bill. 1870. *A Winter in Florida*. New York: Wood and Holbrook.

Martin, Richard A. 1972. *Jacksonville Sesquicentennial, 1822–1972*. Jacksonville: Convention Press.

Mason, Anita, and Diane Packer. 1974. *An Illustrated Dictionary of Jewelry*. Reading, U.K.: Osprey.

McKearin, George, and Helen McKearin. 1941. *American Glassware*. New York: Crown.

Mueller, Edward A. 1980. *Steamboating on the St. Johns, 1830–1885*. Melbourne, Fla.: National Printing.

Mueller, Edward, and Barbara Purdy, eds. 1985. *Conference on the Steamboat Era in Florida*. Gainesville: University of Florida.

Papas, Joan, and A. Harold Kendall. 1971. *Hampshire Pottery Manufactured by J. S. Aft and Company, Keene, New Hampshire*. Manchester, Vt.: Forward's Color Publications.

Papert, Emma. 1972. *The Illustrated Guide to American Glass*. New York: Hawthorne Books.

Pleasants, C. L. 1888. *Official Catalogue, Sub-Tropical Exposition, Jacksonville, Florida*. N.p.

Polk, R. L. 1905. *Jacksonville City Directory*. Jacksonville: Press of Industrial Record.

———. 1907. *Florida Gazetteer and Business Directory 1907–08*. Jacksonville: R. L. Polk.

———. 1911. *Florida Gazetteer and Business Directory 1911–12*. Jacksonville: R. L. Polk.

———. 1918. *Florida Gazetteer and Business Directory 1918–19*. Jacksonville: R. L. Polk.

———. 1925. *Florida Gazetteer and Business Directory 1925–26*. Jacksonville: R. L. Polk.

Rainwater, Dorothy. 1966. *Encyclopedia of American Silver Manufacturers*. West Chester, Pa.: Schiffer.

Rhodes, Harrison, and Mary Wolf Dumont. 1912. *A Guide to Florida for Tourists, Sportsman, and Settlers*. New York: Dodd, Mead.

Richards, Jno. R. *Richards Jacksonville City Directory, 1887*. Jacksonville: J. R. Richards.

Rinhart, Floyd, and Marion Rinhart. 1986. *Victorian Florida*. Atlanta: Peachtree Publishers.

Roberts, Kenneth L. 1926. *Florida*. New York: Harper.

Rohrebacher, Ca. 1887. *Live Towns and Progressive Men*. Jacksonville: Times Union.

Rossen, Howard M. 1998. *World's Fair Collectibles*. Atglen, Pa.: Schiffer.

Sanders, W. Eugene, and Christine C. Sanders. 1997. *Pocket Matchsafes: Reflections of Life and Art, 1840–1920*. Atglen, Pa.: Schiffer.

Smith, Carole, and Richard Smith. 1998. *Antique Shell Decorated Love Tokens—Souvenirs—Whimsies—A Study and Value Guide, Neptune's Treasures*. Huntington, N.Y.: Carole Smith Antiques.

Smith, Charles. 1906. *Jacksonville and Florida Facts, 1905–1906*. Jacksonville: H. and W. B. Drew.

Snyder, Jeffrey B. 1993. *Canes from the Seventeenth to the Twentieth Century*. Atglen, Pa.: Schiffer.

———. 1995. *Historical Staffordshire, American Patriots and Views*. Atglen, Pa.: Schiffer.

St. Augustine City Directory 1911–12. 1911. Richmond, Va.: Polk, 1911.

Stefano, Frank. 1979. *Pictorial Souvenirs and Commemoratives of North America*. New York: Dutton.

Stockbridge, Frank Parker, and John Holliday Perry. 1926. *Florida in the Making*. New York: De Bower.

Stutzenberger, Albert. 1971. *American Historical Spoons: The American Story in Spoons*. Rutland, Vt.: Tuttle.

Sunshine, Silvia. 1880 [1976]. *Petals Plucked from Sunny Climes*. Gainesville: Bicentennial Floridiana Facsimile Series, University Presses of Florida.

Tebeau, Charlton W. 1971. *A History of Florida*. Coral Gables: University of Miami Press.

The Third Annual Descriptive and Statistical Report of the Industries and Advantages of the City of Jacksonville, Florida, 1886. Jacksonville: n.p.

Vance, A. B. 1895. *Vance's Jacksonville Directory 1895*. Jacksonville: Vance.

———. 1898. *Vance's Jacksonville Directory 1898*. Jacksonville: Vance.

———. 1901. *Vance's Jacksonville Directory 1901*. Jacksonville: Vance.

Weaver, Charles. 1927. *Sketches of Jacksonville*. Jacksonville: Bandy.

Webb, W. S. 1876–1877. *Webb's Jacksonville Directory 1876–77*. New York: W. S. Webb.

Weigall, T. H. 1932. *Boom in Paradise*. New York: King.

Westfall, L. Glenn. 1984. *Key West: Cigar City U.S.A.* Key West: Historic Key West Preservation Board.

White, Carole Bess. 1994. *Collector's Guide to Made in Japan Ceramics*. Paducah, Ky.: Collector Books.

White, J. W. 1890. *White's Guide to Florida and Their Famous Resorts*. Jacksonville: DaCosta.

Wiggins, J. 1900. *Jacksonville Directory for 1900*. Jacksonville: East Florida Printing.

———. 1901. *Jacksonville City Directory 1901*. Jacksonville: Wiggins.

———. 1902. *Jacksonville City Directory 1902*. Jacksonville: Wiggins.

———. 1903. *Jacksonville City Directory 1903*. Jacksonville: Wiggins.

———. 1904. *Jacksonville City Directory 1904*. Jacksonville: Wiggins.

Williams, Laurence W. 1998. *Collector's Guide to Souvenir China*. Paducah, Ky.: Collector Books.

Winter, Nevin O. 1918. *Florida, the Land of Enchantment*. Boston: Page.

Index

About the Author

Larry Roberts is a Florida native with a special interest in Florida history. Throughout his childhood and college days he collected fossils and Indian artifacts in central Florida, donating his most significant discoveries to the Florida Museum of Natural History. After acquiring a B.A. in art and a B.S. in anthropology at the University of Florida, he shifted his focus toward antiques. He became interested in early Florida memorabilia about twenty years ago and has actively collected ever since. The illustrations in this book were taken from the author's collection.

Roberts has owned an antique shop in Micanopy for twenty years. He specializes in early Florida memorabilia, art, and antiques. He has written a number of articles on the subject for *Antiques and Art Around Florida*. He welcomes correspondence from fellow enthusiasts or those with questions. He can be reached at P.O. Box 32, Micanopy, Fla. 32667. His e-mail address is buyfl@ atlantic.net.